Socialist History Society
Caribbean Labour Solidarity

Killing Communists in Havana
The Start of the Cold War in Latin America

Steve Cushion

Socialist History
Occasional Publication 39

SOCIALIST
HISTORY
SOCIETY

Published by
The Socialist History Society
and
Caribbean Labour Solidarity

ISBN 978-0-9930104-4-6

Front cover illustration: Jesús Menéndez, General Secretary of the Cuban Sugar Workers' Federation

Contents

Dedicated to the memory of Bel Druce and Sid Kaufman.

Killing Communists in Havana:
The Start of the Cold War in Latin America[1]

On January 22nd 1948, Jesús Menéndez, General Secretary of the National Federation of Sugar Workers, the largest and most important trade union in Cuba, stepped down from a train in the town of Manzanillo and was shot in the back by an army officer. This was the most high profile murder of a trade unionist in Cuba in the late 1940s. He was, however, only one of a dozen workers' leaders who were murdered by soldiers, policemen or gangsters linked to the government and the ruling party. This violent attack on the Cuban trade union movement can be seen as the opening salvoes of the Cold War in Latin America.

Cuba at mid-century

Following US intervention in the Cuban War of Independence (1895-1898) the island received its independence in 1902 but a clause in the new constitution, known as the "Platt Amendment", gave the United States the unilateral right to intervene in Cuban affairs. This constitutional arrangement was accompanied by a Treaty of Reciprocity, which structured economic relations between the two countries to the advantage of the United States. The Platt Amendment was repealed in 1934, following an uprising against the dictatorial regime of President Gerardo Machado, but a new Treaty of Reciprocity was signed that same year, which was even less favourable than the first. In these circumstances, American capital quickly came to dominate the Cuban economy in general and the sugar industry in particular.

The whole Cuban economy was dependent on sugar which provided 80% of the island's exports. The tobacco industry, which was the only other major exporter, had declined considerably, with cigar exports down from 256 million per year in 1906 to only 21 million in 1949. The railway and port infrastructure revolved around the needs of the sugar industry as did the large civil service, which was riddled with corruption. While tourism was expanding, it was largely based on gambling and prostitution and was heavily influenced by the US Mafia. In these circumstances, the island was dominated by the sugar bourgeoisie and the

1   Versions of this paper have been presented to the *London Socialist Historians' Group* in the Institute of Historical research and the *Simposio Internacional "La Revolución Cubana"* in the Palacio de Convenciones, Havana Cuba. The author would like to thank Angelina Rojas, Servando Valdes, Jorge Ibarra Guitart, René Gonzalez Barrios, Belkis Quesada, Josefina Pérez, Pedro Machado and Elvis Rodríguez of the *Institutio de Historia de Cuba*, as well as the staff of the *Archivo Provincial de Las Villas* in Santa Clara, the *Archivo Provincial de Camagüey* and the *Archivo Historico de Sancti Spiritus*. Suggestions for improvements from Ian Birchall, Lesley Catchpowle, Merilyn Moos, Keith Flett, Leonie Jordan, David Morgan and Francis King were also gratefully received.

US banks, with whom they were allied. For most of the first half of the 20th century, the government represented these sugar-based interests to the detriment of industrial development.

There had been a brief period of more enlightened government following the 1933 strikes and army mutiny which removed the authoritarian president Machado, but this was quickly extinguished when the army, working closely with the US ambassador, defeated the general strike of 1935. Initially ruling through puppet presidents and then, from 1940 to 1944 as elected president himself, Fulgencio Batista, the army commander, imposed a regime which combined a mixture of nationalist demagogy and minor social reforms with repression of any attempt by workers to exceed the boundaries established by the government. Following the 1944 elections, he was replaced by governments of the *Partido Revolucionario Cubano - Auténtico* (PRC-A, Cuban Revolutionary Party - Authentic), a liberal nationalist party whose leader, Ramón Grau San Martín, had briefly been president following the 1933 revolution. Despite these revolutionary roots, by the mid-1940s, the *Auténticos*, as the PRC-A was commonly known, was committed to the economic and political status quo, was subservient to the sugar oligarchy and fully accepted Cuba's subordinate relationship with the USA. However, the PRC-A was faced with one of the strongest trade union movements in Latin America.

The labour movement in Cuba has its origins in the guilds and craft unions of the 19th century, but the first nationwide trade union federation, the *Confederación Nacional Obrera de Cuba* (CNOC - Cuban National Labour Confederation), was not founded until 1925. This quickly came to be dominated by the newly formed communist party, the *Partido Comunista de Cuba* (PCC - Communist Party of Cuba). The CNOC did not recover from the defeat of the 1935 general strike and a new trade union centre, the *Confederación de Trabajadores de Cuba* (CTC - Workers Confederation of Cuba), was formed in 1939. By the late 1940s the CTC had the highest percentage of trade unionised workers in Latin America, with over one million members out of a total national population of six million.[2] The Communist Party, now called the *Partido Socialista Popular* (PSP - Popular Socialist Party), was the dominant force in the CTC, with Lázaro Peña, a communist tobacco worker as general secretary.

During the Second World War, in order to gain popular support for its war against Nazi Germany and Fascist Italy, the US government tolerated reformist

---

2   U.S. Embassy Havana, Despatch 1309 (29 June 1955) *Membership of the CTC*

regimes in Latin America that introduced popular welfare measures and granted workers the right to organise. As long as the USSR was an ally of the United States, the Cuban Communist Party remained an acceptable part of the governing coalition. However, the situation changed radically after the defeat of the Axis Powers when the USSR quickly became the new "totalitarian" enemy of the self-designated "Free West". Taking advantage of the changed situation, employers and governments looked for ways to reverse the wartime reforms and to restore profitability in the difficult post-war economic circumstances. The anti-Communist hysteria, which was generated to justify the US change of policy towards the Soviet Union, was also used by the ruling classes in Latin America in an attempt to purge the trade unions of left-wing militants of all political persuasions and to domesticate the remaining leaders, in order to restore a business friendly atmosphere and increase profit margins at the expense of workers' wages and conditions. In the particular circumstances of Cuba in the late 1940s, this involved a mixture of government intervention and gangster violence.

An attack on the Cuban Communists and other militant workers therefore served two purposes: to remove Communist influence and to reduce the ability of the workers to defend the rights and wages gained during the Second World War period. An examination of the background to this assault on the Cuban labour movement unearths a history of government corruption and gangsterism on a level with Al Capone's Chicago. We also find a high level of intervention from the United States, not, as we might suppose, principally from the State Department or the CIA, but from the American Federation of Labor (AFL).

Second World War

Fulgencio Batista, who had been chief of the army and power behind the throne since his forces defeated the 1935 general strike, was elected president of Cuba with Communist support in 1940. The Communists had reached an understanding with Batista whereby, in return for legalisation and some reforms in the interests of the working class, they worked to broaden his narrow social base. One of the outcomes of this arrangement was the establishment of the new trade union federation, the *Confederación de Trabajadores de Cuba* (CTC), which, from its foundation, was dependent on its relationship with the Cuban state. This dependency was increased by the CTC's approach to defending its members' interests, which in most industries relied on the leadership's relationship with the Ministry of Labour, rather than industrial action or collective bargaining. This produced some real improvements for Cuban workers and was part of the process which led to the 1940 constitution, widely recognised as the most progressive in Latin America. Some of the gains made include:

- Paid holidays
- 44 hours work for 48 hours pay
- Reinstatement of workers victimised after the 1935 general strike
- Increased protection from dismissal
- Pension funds in the major industries[3]

The *Partido Socialista Popular* (PSP), as the Cuban Communist Party was known in the 1940s, gained politically by obtaining one third of the seats on the CTC executive and a Communist tobacco worker, Lázaro Peña, was elected General Secretary. This needs to be seen in the context of the Second World War after Pearl Harbour and the German invasion of the Soviet Union when the Communist International relaunched its policy of promoting Popular Fronts against Fascism. The PSP's perception of the importance of defending the USSR meant that, in return for the government's reform package and Cuba's support of the Allied war effort, the CTC worked for national unity and increased productivity. The PSP was also allocated two ministers in Batista's cabinet.

In January 1942, the *Consejo Nacional* (National Council) of the CTC, as part of its commitment to the war effort, voted to "*avoid strikes as far as possible for the duration of the war*".[4] Cuban and North American big business took advantage of this decision to break collective agreements and to ignore those government decrees which they saw as favouring the employees. The system of arbitration, aimed at avoiding strikes, frequently found in favour of the workers but then failed to enforce its rulings. To this must be added the pressure on wages from roaring inflation in basic necessities caused by shortages and speculation. There was a system of price controls, but prices were fixed in consultation with the same merchants who were profiteering from the scarcity and, in any case, there was no mechanism for inspection or enforcement.

Nevertheless, despite the official attitude, in 1943 there was a railway strike in Guantánamo in the extreme east of the island. Those working for the larger railway companies had won a wage rise, decreed by the government, following a campaign which culminated in a very large mass meeting in the *Parque Central* in

---

3   Canton Navarro, *Cuba bajo el signo de la Segunda Guerra Mondial* (n/d) p.52
4   *Hoy* (11 January 1942) [*Hoy* was the daily paper of the PSP]

Havana on 3rd April 1943. The *Ferrocarril de Guantánamo* (Guantánamo Railways) initially refused to pay, leading to a strike which cut off the city of Guantánamo from the rest of the country for a week and also paralysed the local port where the dockers in solidarity refused to load sugar. There was some hostility and suspicion towards this strike from the CTC leadership, firstly because it broke the national no-strike pledge, and secondly because there was a large branch in Guantánamo of the *Partido Obrero Revolucionario* (POR - Workers Revolutionary Party), a group which had split from the communist party in 1930. The initial reaction of the PSP was to condemn the strike as "Trotskyist". Moreover, the congressman for Guantánamo, Eusebio Mujal, was a bitter enemy of the PSP. Mujal had been expelled from the PSP in the early 1930s and had briefly joined the Trotskyist movement. The strike committee went so far as to issue a public leaflet denying any influence from Mujal, repudiating his statements in the press and making it clear that all decisions were taken in mass meetings open to all workers.[5] Despite his suspicion, Ricardo Rodriguez, general secretary of the *Hermandad Ferroviaria* (Railway Brotherhood), intervened with the government on the strikers' behalf and the Guantánamo workers received the same increase as their colleagues in the rest of the country.[6]

Browderism

A more typical example of wartime industrial relations can be seen in the textile industry.[7] In May 1944, the textile employers sought to take advantage of a court ruling that some of the government's social protection legislation was unconstitutional to resist paying a wage increase.[8] The CTC's first response was to call for continued co-operation between employers and workers, avoiding stoppages of production, supporting the call from the *Asociación Nacional de Industriales de Cuba* (ANIC - National Association of Industrialists) for "an atmosphere of peace and harmony".[9] The Ministry of Labour brokered negotiations throughout July, but by the end of August the employers were clearly not willing to pay. A strike was called, then postponed following further meetings at the Ministry.[10] There were further negotiations throughout September, while workplace meetings and a mass rally increased pressure for an increase. On 27th

---

5   *Archivo Nacional de Cuba, Fondo Especial 9-17-1601* (18 May 1943)
6   Zanetti & García, *Caminos para el azúcar* (1987) p.347
     and there were daily accounts of the strike in the local newspaper *Voz del Pueblo*
7   I am grateful to Pedro Machado of the *Instituto de Historia de Cuba* for sight of his unpublished manuscript.
8   *Hoy* (23 June 1944)
9   *Hoy* (29 June 1944)
10 *Hoy* (29 August 1944, 23 September 1944)

September 1944, the textile union executive called for a strike and demonstration for the 1st October, but postponed it for 10 days following a request from the president who finally issued two decrees on the 3rd and 7th October enforcing a wage rise, although the Communist press was vague as to the exact amount of the increase, so it may not have been paid in full.[11]

The Cuban Communists, along with many other Communist Parties in Latin America, were heavily influenced by the Communist Party USA (CPUSA) which, at this time, was led by Earl Browder. Browder took the class collaboration implicit in the idea of a Popular Front to the extreme and advocated peaceful co-existence between capital and labour as part of a wider peace between the USA and the USSR. He wrote:

> *We frankly declare that we are ready to cooperate in making this capitalism work effectively in the postwar period with the least possible burdens upon the people.[12]*

The Cuban adoption of a similar line is demonstrated in a speech given by Lázaro Peña, General Secretary of the CTC and member of the executive of the PSP at a banquet given by the ANIC, the main association of employers in sectors other than sugar. This was published as a pamphlet entitled *Colaboración entre Obreros y Patronos* (Collaboration between workers and bosses) and argued for collaboration in the interests of the national economy to continue after the war.

However, Browder did not foresee the changes that were coming about as the war was drawing to a close and an Allied victory seemed to be only a matter of time. In 1944, he proposed that the US Communist Party be wound up and replaced with a "Communist Political Association", a step too far for both the government of the Soviet Union and many members of the CPUSA itself. When Jacques Duclos, a leading member of the French CP, widely interpreted as speaking on behalf of Stalin, wrote an open letter heavily criticising the politics of the North American party, Browder's enemies, led by William Z Foster, removed him from office in June 1945 and quickly expelled him. The Cuban Communists formally renounced *Browderism* in January 1946 when Foster, now leader of the CPUSA, addressed the Third National Assembly of the PSP.[13] This change of policy inevitably took some time to be accepted by the party membership, which had grown from 4,756 in 1937 to 65,324 in 1944, so the new political situation

---

11 *Hoy* (10 October 1944)
12 Duclos , *On the Dissolution of the Communist Party of the United States* (1945)
13 *Hoy* (26 January 1946)

was outside the experience of most members who would have joined when the party was part of the government coalition.[14] However, the Communists were not the only ones looking towards a changed postwar situation.

US president Franklin Roosevelt had been unhappy with the fact that Batista had included two Communist ministers in his government; legalising the CP in return for their support of the war effort was tolerable, having them in the cabinet was not. Thus, when Batista's term of office came to an end in 1944, the US Office of Naval Intelligence (ONI) used Meyer Lansky, a Mafia gangster with business interests in Cuba, as a go-between to quietly tell Batista that the US government did not wish him to seek re-election.[15] The 1944 elections were won by Ramón Grau San Martín, who was an anti-Communist but, given that he did not have a majority in the House of Representatives, needed Communist votes in parliament.[16] However, this did not stop him from preparing to drive the Communists out of the CTC.

The American Federation of Labor

In the late 1940s the ruling party in Cuba, the *Partido Auténtico* (PRC-A), had become a byword for corruption. Its two most prominent leaders were Ramón Grau San Martín, who served as president of Cuba from 1933 to 1934 as well as from 1944 to 1948, and Carlos Prío Socarrás who was president from 1948 to 1952. With the encouragement of Grau and Prío, supporters of the *Autenticos*, as the PRC-A was known, had been organising in the CTC from the outset but, given their initial lack of working class support, they had found it convenient to come to an arrangement with the PSP which gave them a number of seats on the executive. The position was further complicated by the fact that many *Autentico* trade unionists were genuinely prepared to work with the PSP leadership. Within the CTC, the grouping of Communists and the faction of the *Autenticos* prepared to work alongside them, as well as many sympathetic independent unionists, referred to themselves as "*unitarios*". The anti-Communist *Auténticos* organised themselves into the *Comisión Obrera Nacional Auténtica* (CON(A) - National Workers Commission of the *Autentico* Party).

The first attempt to split the CTC took place at the Third Congress in December 1942, but delegates from only 45 of a total of 961 local unions walked out, with many important anti-Communists not yet ready to show their hand, most

---

14 Rojas Blaquier, *El Primer Partido Comunista de Cuba , tomo 2* (2006) p.58
15 Colhoun , *Gangsterismo, The United States, Cuba, and the Mafia: 1933 to 1966* (2013) p.9
16 National Archives (UK), FO 371/44411 - AN 1103 (1945) *President Grau attitude to Communists*

significant of whom was Juán Arévalo of the *Federación de Obreros Marítimos Nacional* (FOMN - National Federation of Maritime Workers). However, in July 1943, at the instigation of the US government's Office of Inter-American Affairs (OIAA), headed by Nelson Rockefeller, the American Federation of Labor (AFL) invited Juán Arévalo to the USA and begin a new phase of their interference in the Cuban labour movement.

The AFL had been anti-socialist from the beginning, placing the interest of the union bureaucracy over any notion of workers' solidarity, a position exemplified by the sell-out of the American Railroad Union strike of 1894. Samuel Gompers, founding leader of the AFL, had been particularly concerned by competition from the Industrial Workers of the World (IWW) and wholeheartedly supported President Woodrow Wilson's ruthless campaign of state repression against them. In 1916, Gompers represented "labour" on the Council of National Defence, the body aimed at putting the US economy on a war footing and, in 1917, at government behest, tried to get Mexico to join the war on the US side. Aware that the IWW was recruiting in Mexico, he helped set up the Pan American Federation of Labor (PAFL) in an alliance with the Mexican trade union federation, the *Confederación Regional Obrera Mexicana* (CROM - Regional Confederation of Mexican Workers). This international initiative had help from the US government via $50,000 from the president's "special fund", thus setting a pattern of collaboration between the AFL and the US state which continues to this day. The PAFL quickly turned its attention to combating Communism which now replaced the IWW as the main "Red menace". With the death of Gompers in 1927, the AFL lost interest in Latin America until the Second World War, when they again offered their services to the US government. The AFL worked for industrial peace and productivity and was rewarded with positions on government committees, including areas of foreign policy. It was through this collaboration in foreign affairs that Serafino Romualdi first appears on the scene.

Romualdi was an anti-Communist Italian Social Democrat who had fled to the USA following the rise of Mussolini. During the war he worked for the Office of Strategic Services (OSS) in Italy helping to build a moderate labour-based resistance outside of and in competition with the mainstream Communist-led partisan movement. Sometime in 1943 or 1944 he transferred to the Office of Inter-American Affairs for whom, under the auspices of the International Ladies' Garment Workers' Union (ILGWU) and the AFL, he made tours of Latin America, although this role was not made public until, in February 1946, an article in the

New York Times announced his appointment as the AFL special representative in Latin America.[17] In April 1947, Romualdi met a number of senior State Department officials and noted that "*the attitude of the State Department towards our efforts to combat Communist and other totalitarian influences in Latin America will from now on be not only sympathetic but cooperative*".[18] Phillip Agee described him as the "*principal CIA agent for labour operations in Latin America*".[19] His main task for both his employers was to destroy the CTAL.

The *Confederacion de Trabajadores de America Latina* (CTAL - Workers Confederation of Latin America) was formed in 1938 and headed by the Mexican Vicente Lombardo Toledano. It was set up as an international trade union federation to unite all workers in Latin America but, because it contained Communist led as well as non-Communist union federations and Lombardo Toledano was considered a "fellow traveller", it earned the enmity of the AFL. Not that it was hostile to the Allied war effort, quite the contrary, many of Lombardo Toledano's speeches are reminiscent of "Browderism".[20] The CTAL was very much part of the Popular Front and the US State Department did not want this disturbed until after an Allied victory. Nevertheless, the AFL was politically to the right of the State Department and anticipated the coming Cold War before it became government policy. The union bureaucracy clearly planned to be well placed to assist the future turn in US foreign policy.[21] Romualdi saw the Cuban CTC as a crucial battleground and worked to prepare the ground.

The Split

In 1944, the US State Department was still keen to maintain the wartime alliance and the *Comisión Obrera Nacional Auténtica* (CON(A)) was discouraged from causing trouble at the Fourth Congress of the CTC in December. Agreement was reached to share the major offices on the executive, with an *Autentico* deputy to a Communist office holder and vice versa. Lázaro Peña was re-elected General Secretary, while leading members of the CON(A) were elected to important positions such as Francisco Aguirre of the restaurant workers' federation as Organising Secretary and Emilio Surí Castillo of the sugar workers as Correspondence Secretary as well as Juan Arévalo of the dock workers' union as

---

17 Buchanan , *"Useful Fools" as Diplomatic Tools* (1990) p. 5
18 Romualdi, *Presidents and Peons* (1967) pp.72-3
19 Agee, *Inside the Company* (1975) p.544
20 Roxborough, *Labor Control and the Postwar Growth Model in Latin America* (1994) p.253
21 Buchanan , *"Useful Fools" as Diplomatic Tools* (1990) p. 13

Secretary for Foreign Relations.[22] Suri Castillo made it quite clear by his repeated public attacks on his Communist fellow executive members that he did not see the agreement lasting.[23]

Juan Arévalo was a frequent visitor to the US Embassy and the diplomatic reports indicate that he continued working closely with the AFL, using the Embassy as a postbox.[24] Describing himself as a "moderate socialist", Arévalo was highly critical of the Communists in his own union for refusing to accept wage cuts after the war, along with an "intensification of the efficiency and productivity of Cuban workers", which he felt was necessary if Cuba were to be attractive to foreign capital investment. He also expressed admiration for Spruille Braden, the US Ambassador to Cuba, who was notorious for his anti-union views and his long term association with the United Fruit Company.[25] Given the high level of United Fruit investment in Cuba, Braden clearly had both commercial as well as political interests in increased productivity in Cuba and Juan Arévalo was therefore likely have been doubly useful.

In September 1945, Arévalo, accompanied by Francisco Aguirre and Eusebio Mujal, the *Autentico* congressman from Guantánamo, visited Washington as an official delegation from president Grau. They had meetings with various State Department officials and with Sidney Green, AFL president, with whom they discussed the idea of forming a new international trade union federation for Latin America that would exclude the Communists. In January 1946, Sidney Green proposed a tour of Latin America by a group of anti-Communist trade union leaders and Arévalo, accompanied by Francisco Aguirre attended a specially convened meeting of the AFL executive in Miami to make arrangements. This was reported in the Miami local newspapers and Arévalo told the Havana newspaper *El Mundo* that he favoured a new international organisation. Following their visit, the two union officials were faced with a CTC disciplinary enquiry, but their explanations were accepted in the name of "unity", although probably not believed.[26] Arévalo, despite his assurances to the contrary, maintained his links with the State Department, reporting to Spruille Braden, who was now Assistant Secretary of State for American Republic Affairs, during his tour of the Caribbean.

The mid-term parliamentary elections in June 1946 gave President Grau a

22 Tellería Toca , *Congresos obreros en Cuba* (1973) pp. 337-349
23 Embassy of the USA (21 June 1945) Airmail Number 95280 - *Autentico Labor Leader Voices Attack on Communists*
24 Embassy of the USA (27 February 1945, 10 April 1945, 14 September 1945 amongst others)
25 Embassy of the USA (10 April 10 1945) *Conversation with Juan Arevalo*
26 *Revista CTC* (February 1946) "Resolución del XI Consejo Nacional de la CTC sobre relaciones de Francisco Aguirre con la 'American Federation of Labour '", p.11

comfortable majority in the House of Representatives where he no longer needed the votes of the Communist deputies. In February 1947, Grau made a speech at a banquet organised by the CON(A) calling on Cubans to "abandon foreign doctrines"; this was widely interpreted as encouraging the CON(A) to move against the Communists in the CTC, although the PSP did not finally withdraw support from the government until September of that year.[27] Throughout the takeover of the CTC, president Grau played his cards very close to his chest, privately assuring the British and US embassies that he was a stern anti-Communist and encouraging CON(A) in their takeover bid, but publicly calling for unity and saying that he could not interfere.

The Fifth Congress of the CTC was scheduled to take place in December 1946, but was postponed until the following April. The CON(A) used the delay to win support amongst an "independent" faction within the CTC bureaucracy led by Angel Cofiño, general secretary of the electrical workers' federation. On 3rd April 1947, less than a week before the congress was due to start, a group of gangsters opened fire with pistols on the PSP offices, although no-one was hurt.[28] Then on 5th April there were more shooting attacks on three PSP neighbourhood committee offices which left three people wounded.[29] Meanwhile, Francisco Aguirre of the restaurant workers' federation, as secretary of the credentials commission, refused to recognise the credentials of a number of delegates known to support the PSP who, in turn, challenged many of the CON(A) supporters. In this fractious atmosphere, Emilio Surí Castillo, who was secretary of the CON(A) and a leading member of the *Federación Nacional de Trabajadores Azucareros* (FNTA - National Federation of Sugar Workers), a man with a history of violence against political opponents, led a march to the offices of the *Sindicato de los Obreros de la Aguja* (textile workers), where the credentials were kept, in an attempt to seize the conference papers. In the fight that followed one member of the CON(A), Félix Palú, was killed and a PSP member wounded. The Minister of Labour, Carlos Prío Socarrás, used this as an excuse to suspend the congress and appointed a new credentials commission, with Francisco Aguirre representing the CON(A), Manuel Zorilla for the independents (also known as CON-I) and José Morera for the "*unitarios*".[30] The following evening, police raided the CTC offices and arrested several people, including the Havana dockers' leader Aracelio Iglesias, on

---

27 FO 371/60879 - AN 988 (21 February 1947) Political Situation in Cuba
    FO 371/60879 - AN 1711 (26 April 1947) Political Situation in Cuba
    PCC, *Historia del movimiento obrero cubano* II (1985) p.186
28 *Hoy* (4, 5 April 1947)
29 *Hoy* (6 April 1947)
30 *Hoy* (6 April 1947)

trumped up charges of possession of arms. CTC General Secretary Lázaro Peña went to the presidential palace to protest, but President Grau reassured him that his sole interest was to ensure a safe and successful congress. [31]

The anti-Communist representatives on the official credentials commission dragged their feet and it still had not reported a month later. Following a successful and well attended May Day rally, Lázaro Peña decided not to wait for the credentials report and the CTC executive convened the Fifth Congress on the 4th May. President Grau hypocritically sent a message of greetings.[32] About ¾ of the labour movement responded, 923 local unions sending 1403 delegates.[33] The leadership of the CON(A) and the independents called for a boycott, although this was ignored by some 300 *Autentico* delegates.[34]

Despite this seeming victory for the *unitarios*, Minister of Labour Carlos Prío was working behind the scenes with Eusebio Mujal, who soon became the effective leader of the CON(A). Mujal had never been a worker, but was an ex-Communist, ex-Trotskyist, now *Autentico* parliamentary representative from Guantánamo (although it is said that he was born in Barcelona). He did not allow this to stand in his way; his political connections, personal corruption and murderous ruthlessness amply compensated for his lack of a base in the trade union movement. The CON(A) and the CON-I jointly organised their own congress on 6th July 1947 in Radio-Cine in the Havana suburb of Vedado, which elected the "independent" leader of the electrical workers federation, Angel Cofiño, as general secretary. News magazine *Bohemia* subsequently exposed the fact that the Ministry of Education had financed this congress with $40,000 from its fund "K", which was intended to pay for primary education. [35] The government then moved swiftly against the *unitarios* and on 29th July police and soldiers expelled them from the CTC headquarters, the *Palacio de los Trabajadores* (Workers' Palace).[36] There were protest strikes all over the country, but they were frequently symbolic, lasting only 5 or 10 minutes, while Lázaro Peña protested to the president.[37]

Francisco Aguirre and Eusebio Mujal went immediately to Washington with a message from President Grau and there met the Assistant Secretary of State for

---

31 *Hoy* (8 April 1947)
32 *Hoy* (4 May 1947)
33 Hoy (6 May 1947)
34 FO 371/60879 - AN 2176 (12 May 1947) *Control of CTC*
35 *Bohemia* (13 July 1947) "Otro V Congreso" pp.49 & 54 [*Bohemia* was a weekly Cuban news magazine]
36 *Hoy* (30 July 1947)
     Bohemia (3 August 1947) "Deslojo del Palacio de los Trabajadores"
37 FO 371/60879 - AN 3196 (2 September 1947) *Control of the Cuban Labour Movement*

Interamerican Affairs as well as Serafino Romualdi, to whom they promised the support of the CTC for an anti-Communist Interamerican trade union conference.[38] The Ministry of Labour then decreed, on October 9th, that the May CTC congress, which had elected Lázaro Peña, was null and void, and that the July congress was legally recognised. Given that the Cuban Constitution recognised only one union confederation, Prío gave formal recognition to Angel Cofiño as General Secretary of the CTC and passed him the keys of the *Palacio de los Trabajadores*.[39] Lázaro Peña immediately issued a call for protest strikes which received support from the Havana dock workers, many tobacco workers and the capital's bus and tram drivers.[40] On the 15th, the CTC called for a four hour protest strike to which the government responded with considerable brutality and hundreds of arrests, at the same time as closing down the PSP radio station *Mil Diez*.[41] This repression broke the strike demonstrating the limits of "protest" in the face of determined state action.

Having taken over the CTC, the Ministry of Labour moved against the *unitarios* in the constituent federations. The CON(A) already controlled the electrical workers' and the telephone workers' federations; they used a mixture of government intervention and corruption to take over the official structures of the other unions, while a number of *unitario* bureaucrats, seeing where their personal best interests lay, changed sides. These interventions did not prove to be a great problem for the government in those unions where the officers had solely relied on their good relations with local or national officials of the Ministry of Labour to get advances for their members; these had little experience in organising mass action, just the occasional short protest strike or demonstration to push a tardy civil servant into action. However, there were other industries with a much greater tradition of self activity; these would prove a harder nut to crack and would require more brutal measures. In these areas gangsters linked to the *Auténticos* used violence to enforce the change of officials.

Gangsterismo

From the early days of the Cuban Republic, the domination of economic life

---

38 Department of State Memorandum of Conversation (31 July 1947) *Visit of Cuban Auténtico Labor Leaders*
     Romualdi, *Presidents and Peons : Recollections of a Labor Ambassador in Latin America* (1967) pp 65 & 75
     FO 371/60879 - AN 3196 (2 September 1947) *Control of the Cuban Labour Movement*
39 FO 371/60879 - AN 3805 (29 October 1947) *Cuban Labour Movement*
     Hoy (10 October 1947)
40 *Hoy* (14 October 1947)
41 FO 371/60879 - AN 3805 (29 October 47) *Cuban Labour Movement*
     Hoy (15, 16, 17 October 1947)

by US big business had left little space for would-be Cuban entrepreneurs, many of whom turned to politics to make money. José Miguel Gómez, the second president of Cuba from 1909 to 1913 began the process of institutionalising graft and he was a millionaire by the end of his term of office. When the 1929 Crash caused a catastrophic fall in the price of sugar and the Cuban economy suffered a severe depression, workers and the unemployed took to the streets. This political/economic elite was determined to retain its power and privileges, with the result that President Gerardo Machado, who had recently arranged his own fraudulent re-election, repressed the protests. Not only did he use the Police and Army to shoot down demonstrators, he set up unofficial death squads, known as *porristas* (literally "cheerleaders"), to murder his opponents. Anti-Machado groups set up their own action groups, armed self-defence and vengeance squads, and there were frequent gun battles between pro and anti-regime gunmen on the streets of Havana.

Machado was removed by the 1933 revolution but, following the 1935 counter-revolution led by Batista, these action groups, most of whom had very little politics outside of a visceral hatred of Machado and his goons, lost their way. By the time Batista left office in 1944, these gangs of *pistoleros* were enmeshed in political corruption, working as enforcers for different factions in the political elite and operating protection rackets, although they kept the revolutionary sounding names they had adopted during the fight against Machado. They were mainly based in Havana University, posing as "student leaders", and as they frequently fell out over the spoils, the University became the scene of numerous gunfights and assassinations.

During the late 1940s when the *Autentico* party dominated Cuban politics, presidents Ramon Grau San Martín (1944-48) and Carlos Prío Socarrás (1948-52) embedded gangsterism and corruption in Cuban political and social life. In 1950, then ex-President Grau was accused of embezzling $174 million, but the matter never came to court because, in the early hours of July 4th 1950, a group of gunmen arrived at the court and took away all the court papers and evidence in the case.[42] Members of two gangs, the *Movimiento Socialista Revolucionaria* (MSR - Revolutionary Socialist Movement) and the *Unión Insurreccional Revolucionaria* (UIR - Revolutionary Insurrectional Union) became embedded in the police force under Grau's Presidency. This erupted into a scandal in September 1947, known as the *Orfila* affaire, when police led by the Director of the Special Investigation

---

42 *New York Times* (5 July 1950)
    Hoy (5 July 1950)

Service of the National Police, Mario Salabría of the MSR, surrounded the house of the Director of the Police Academy, Emilio Tró of the UIR, claiming he was wanted for murder of a police captain who had been a member of the MSR. There followed a two hour gunfight which left six dead; the two factions of police were finally separated by the Army.[43]

Much of the corruption under president Grau was organised by José Manuel Aléman, his Minister of Education. In the fallout of the *Orfila* affair, the army raided Aléman's country house, where they found thirteen lorryloads of arms and ammunition, including .50 calibre machine guns. At Aléman's swearing in ceremony, known members of the MSR and another gang called *Acción Revolucionaria Guiteras* (ARG) were present and took part in the celebrations.[44] In fact, such was the familiarity with these gangsters in presidential circles that, throughout the terms of both Grau and Prío, they were known in the presidential Palace as "*Los Muchachos*" (The Boys).[45] Education in Cuba was funded by *Inciso K* (Paragraph K) of a decree issued in December 1943, which taxed 9 centavos on every bag of sugar exported and assigned it to the Ministry of Education. Aléman would use this money to fund the *Autentico* mid-term election victory in 1946 and to employ a private army of thugs in sinecure positions, as well as enriching himself and other members of the government including the president. This fund "K" was used to fund the split in the CTC and, for this reason, the official CTC led by Cofiño and later Mujal was often called the "CTK". Meanwhile, the national illiteracy rate was still 23% in 1953.

But it was President Carlos Prío who raised *gangsterismo* to a method of government.[46] He had particularly close links with a gang called *Acción Revolucionaria Guiteras* (ARG) who did much of the dirty work of removing those *unitario* CTC leaders who would not go quietly and who could not be bought; a task facilitated by Prío giving ARG leader Eufemio Fernández a job as head of the *Policía Secreta Nacional* (National Secret Police) and appointing Jesús González Cartas (aka *El Extraño*), another prominent ARG hoodlum, as Chief of the *Policía Marítima del Puerto de La Habana* (Maritime Police of the Port of Havana).[47]

ARG were alone among the Cuban gangsters of the period to have an ideology

43 *Hoy* (16 September 1947)
    New York Times (16 September 1947)
44 U.S. Embassy Havana, Despatch 1882 (May 9, 1946) *Jose Manuel Aleman*
45 *Bohemia* (24 June 1951)
46 Pardrón & Betancourt, *Batista, el golpe* (2013) pp.30-36
47 Colhoun, *Gangsterismo* (2013) pp.14-16

of sorts. They saw themselves as heirs to the tradition of Antonio Guiteras, a leading opponent of the Machado dictatorship in the 1930s who had been killed in the repression following the defeat of the 1935 general strike. He had briefly served as a Minister during the 1933 revolution and was responsible for many reforms such as the minimum wage. A socialist and anti-imperialist nationalist, he was however much influenced by anarchist ideas of "propaganda by the deed". The ARG had degenerated a very long way from the idealism of Guiteras, but selective quotations from this revolutionary hero gave the ARG the excuse to inflict as much violence as they wished on their enemies. Their political front did indeed trick some people who normally had sounder judgement, as shown by the sympathetic article about them in the normally perceptive news magazine *Bohemia*.[48] In the name of preventing crime and suppressing the *pistoleros*, Prío appointed 2000 gang members to jobs in the civil service, many in the police. He was probably less personally corrupt than Grau; the British Ambassador estimated that he had stolen a mere $90 million when he left office.[49]

Carlos Prío had two brothers, Paco and Antonio. FBI reports say that Paco, who served as a Senator from 1944 to 1952, was a drug dealer and a gambler, a close friend of the Mafia bosses, Meyer Lansky and Lucky Luciano.[50] Antonio served as *Ministerio de la Hacienda* (Finance Minister) from where he was widely reported to have embezzled vast sums from the workers' pension funds.[51] Corruption was also at the heart of the motive for the involvement of so many gangsters in the takeover of the unions. The retirement funds set up during and immediately after the Second World War contained millions of dollars and were ripe for corrupt exploitation. Thus, for example, December 1949 saw reports that $200,000 was missing from the tram workers' retirement fund.[52] The real prize was the sugar workers' retirement fund. In October 1949, Conrado Rodriquez, regional sugar workers' leader from Las Villas who had once been a member of ARG but broke with them when their criminal nature became obvious, started a campaign that accused Mujal and Surí Castillo of pillaging the fund of $9 million. By September 1951, the missing funds totalled $16 million. He continued this campaign through 1956, when he placed evidence of Mujal's embezzlement from the fund before the court and finally, on January 24th 1960 presented his collected

---

48 *Bohemia* (27 July 1947) "Acción Revolucionaria Guiteras"
49 *Alerta* (4 March 1952) [*Alerta* was a Cuban newspaper of the period]
     Ameringer, *The Cuban Democratic Experience: the Auténtico Years, 1944-1952* (2000) p.177
50 Colhoun, *Gangsterismo, The United States, Cuba, and the Mafia: 1933 to 1966* (2013) pp.15-16
51 *Bohemia* (16 October 1949) "El dinero físico ha desaparecido";
52 Hoy (29 December 1949, 7 January 1950, 14 October 1956)
     U.S. Embassy Havana, Despatch 212 (January 31, 1950) *Labor Notes on Havana, Jan. 11-30, 1950*

evidence of the corrupt handling of the fund to Che Guevara who was then Minister of the Economy after the victory of the revolution. [53]

In this atmosphere, a new, anti-corruption party, the *Partido del Pueblo Cubano - Ortodoxo* (Party of the Cuban People - Orthodox, commonly known as the *Ortodoxos*), was founded in 1947 by a breakaway from the *Auténticos* led by Senator Eduardo Chibás. The main plank of their election platform was opposition to corruption allied to a vaguely expressed economic nationalism, which called for recovery of national wealth and promised to implement measures of social equality. Chibás himself had a weekly radio programme which, until his suicide in 1951, he used to expose government corruption and to attack its links with organised crime. Indeed, Chibás alleged that collaboration between the Prío brothers and Ramon Grau was behind the theft of the court papers in the case against Grau and the missing $174 million, as all concerned had too much to lose if the truth came out.[54]

One of the services that these gangsters provided their political masters was the assassination of trade unionists who could not be corrupted. Among those union leaders murdered in this fashion were three of the most respected Communist workers' leaders, the docker, Aracelio Iglesias, the cigar-roller Miguel Fernández Roig and the sugar worker, Jésus Menéndez. But the violence first started in earnest on the buses.

Public Transport

Public transport in Havana had been a stronghold of the *Partido Socialista Popular* and the struggle for control of the union was particularly vicious in this sector. This battle between the *unitarios* and the gangsters of ARG was complicated the machinations of a corrupt US businessman, who was also working for the CIA. In the resulting "Havana Public Transport Scandal of 1950", we see the coming together of the corruption, murder, gangsterism, business interests and Cold War politics that typifies the late 1940s and early 1950s in Cuba.

Marco Hirigoyen, a leading member of the ARG, gained control of the transport workers' union in a particularly ruthless manner. On 27th October 1947, following a peaceful demonstration by bus drivers outside the Ministry of Labour, a large group went to the offices of the Communist daily newspaper *Hoy* to request that their story be printed the next day.[55] When they arrived, the police,

---

53 *Bohemia* (16 October 1949, 30 September 195, 14 October 1956, 24 January 1960)
54 *Bohemia* (9 June 1950) "En el madrugada del 4 de Julio"; (23 July 1950) "Chibás vuelve a urgencia"
55 *Hoy* (28 October) 1947)

commanded by Comandante Azcuí, opened fire with no warning and three bus workers were wounded, one of whom, Anton Lezcano, later died.[56] Two days later, police and Ministry of Labour officials ejected the elected leadership from the union offices of the bus company *Autobuses Aliados* and gave the premises to the official CTC led by Angel Cofiño. On 10th November 1947, Manuel Montoro, a leading Communist activist on the buses was shot down in a café by gunmen from *Acción Revolucionaria Guiteras*.[57] On the 3rd December, three tram drivers who were loyal to the PSP union leadership were wounded in a shooting attack.[58] On 11th April 1948, a rank and file Communist Hector Cabrera was killed by ARG gunmen while in conversation with colleagues at the terminus.[59] Marco Hirigoyen used this wave of assassinations to remove and intimidate his political opponents and take over the transport union. The Havana Electric Tramway Company then made 200 jobs available to ARG mobsters, with the intention of ensuring the domination of the ARG over the workforce, by threats of violence if necessary. Unwelcome attention was drawn to this when two factions of the ARG quarrelled over the rake-off they were demanding from their own associates to fill the places, a dispute which ended in a gunfight that had to be broken up by the police.[60] Hirigoyen himself was a friend of the Catholic priest Padre Enrique Oslé, leader of the *Juventud Obrera Católica* (JOC - Catholic Labour Youth - a Social-Christian organisation), and was greatly attracted to the right-wing, working class populism of the Peronist trade unions in Argentina. He used the base he had created on the Havana buses to promote his own career in the official CTC, becoming a member of the executive at the Sixth Congress in April 1949.

By 1950, the Havana tram system was on its last legs.[61] The government had acquired control of the Havana Electric Railway Company in 1948 to rescue it from the financial problems that its owners, the US owned electricity supply companies, had proved unwilling or incapable of solving.[62] Meanwhile, the communist newspaper, *Hoy*, was printing stories of corruption by the government and their allies in the transport union, alleging that the $200,000 missing from the retirement fund was being used to buy new overhead cables.[63]

A US businessman, ex-diplomat and owner of the Miami Beach Railway

---

56 *Hoy* (13, 14, 15 November 1947)
57 *Hoy* (11 November 1947)
58 *Hoy* (3 December 1947)
59 *Hoy* (11 April 1948)
60 *Hoy* (9 June 1948)
61 *Hoy* (3 January 1950)
62 *Bohemia* (January 8 1950) "El grave problema tranviario"
63 *Hoy* (4, 5, 12 January 1950)

Company and the Miami Transit Company, William Pawley, concluded an agreement with the government to replace the dilapidated tram system with a fleet of new buses. Under the terms of this agreement, he would supply £2,500,000 and another £5,000,000 would be in the form of a loan from the Royal Bank of Canada. A further $2,500,000 would be raised from local investors. The new company, to be known as *Autobuses Modernos*, would take over the property, obligations and employees of the Havana Electric Railway and would acquire 720 new, British-built buses to run the service.[64]

It was also agreed, although not publicly, that the new company would discharge 2000 of the currently employed 5000 employees of Havana Electric;[65] the potential threat to jobs was however obvious to the employees, who were also concerned about the financial viability of their retirement scheme.[66] Marco Hirigoyen and the ARG union leadership were, however, satisfied following a meeting with William Pawley, who promised to respect existing collective agreements and replenish the retirement fund with 25% of the new company's profits. On the other hand, a leaflet issued in the name of the *Comité de Defensa de los Obreros y Empleados Tranviarios* (Tram Workers' Defence Committee), an opposition grouping within the union that was led by members of the *Partido Socialista Popular*, alleged that the union leadership was paid $50,000 for their agreement.[67] Coincidentally, Pawley told the British Embassy that the only liability he inherited from the Havana Electric Railway was $50,000 to pay a local tax known as the "*censo*".[68] Be this as it may, this promised attitude by the new director was in sharp contrast with the existing industrial relations, there having just been a strike which involved strikebreaking by the police, who managed to wreck a number of trams and injure some of the unfortunate passengers.[69]

Negotiations to buy a fleet of new buses from the British manufacturer Leyland Motors began at the end of January 1950.[70] Pawley ran into almost immediate financial trouble as he counted upon discounting bills representing his

64 U.S. Embassy Havana, *Despatch 328* (13 February 1950)
    "Havana en vias de solucionar uno de sus grandes problemas" *Bohemia* (5 March 1950) pp.68-70
    Hoy (17 February 1950)
65 U.S. Embassy Havana, *Despatch 543* (March 9 1950)
66 *Hoy* (2 March 1950)
67 Comité de Defensa de los Obreros y Empleados Tranviarios (15 March 1950) *Llamamiento a los Obreros y Empleados Tranviarios* [copy in author's possession]
68 FO 371/81476 - AK1372/3 (7 February 1950) *Sale of Leyland Buses to Cuba*
69 *Bohemia (*March 12, 1950) "Tranviario el problema" and "Editorial"
    Hoy (8 March 1950)
70 FO 371/81476 - AK1372/1 (25 January 1950) *Sale of Leyland Buses to Omnibuses Modernos*
    FO 371/81476 - AK1372/2 (2 February 1950) *Further negotiations about proposed sale of British Buses to Cuba*
    FO 371/81476 - AK1372/3 (7 February 1950) *Sale of Leyland Buses to Cuba*

commission with Royal Bank of Canada before the buses were shipped. When that did not prove possible, he asked the British for a loan based on his commission. The Treasury agreed to accept liability for up to £1m.[71] With a fanfare of publicity, Route A, from Vlboro to Vedado was launched in July 1950; four more routes were added during the course of the month.[72] However, the honeymoon between William Pawley and his employees did not last long, ending in a public argument in the press between the union and management, with Pawley accusing the workers of stealing the fares and damaging the buses. He further accused the union of failing to facilitate a purge of communists from the workforce.[73] The real difference between management and union appears to have been a question of staffing levels, seniority for training and scheduling flexibility. A mass meeting voted for a strike on October 23rd. Faced with the obvious displeasure of the President of the Republic and a large mobilisation of police, the General Secretary of the CTC persuaded the leader of the union at *Autobuses Modernos*, Marco Hiragoyen, to return to negotiations.[74]

Despite the quasi-fascist methods employed by the Grau and Prío governments to purge the unions, Cuba was, until Batista's coup in March 1952, still technically a democracy with some semblance of the rule of law. In these circumstances, Hirigoyen and his associates in the ARG, had to maintain a measure of popular support amongst the rank and file workers. This entailed defending jobs and conditions, although frequently from a reactionary and populist political position. For instance, the ARG argued in support of a fare increase on the grounds that it was necessary to ensure that the company could afford existing staffing and wage levels. The minority of transport workers who opposed this and argued for an alliance with the passengers against management were subject to violent intimidation. On 20th October 1948 a young Communist bus driver, Carlos Febles, who was active in the campaign to oppose the proposed fare increase, was shot dead while sleeping on his bus at the terminus.[75] It was this need to maintain a level of support amongst the tram and bus crews that led Hirigoyen into a confrontation with William Pawley.

As the end of 1950 approached, not only did Pawley have to face industrial relations problems, the obscure financing of the business began to unravel. The

71 FO 371/81476 - AK1372/4 (23 February 1950) *Leylands - Cuba*
72 U.S. Embassy Havana, *Despatch 148* (21 July 1950)
    Bohemia (16, 30 July, 6 August)
73 U.S. Embassy Havana, *Despatch 506* (1 September 1950)
    Hoy (29 August 1950)
74 "Trabajo" *Bohemia* (29 October 1948)
75 *Hoy* (21 October 1948)

Minister of Finance, Pepin Bosch, probably the only honest finance minister in the pre-1959 Cuban Republic, explained that the cheque for $500,000 that his department sent to *Autobuses Modernos* was to buy 5000 preferential shares in the company on behalf of the government. William Pawley, on the other hand, in a letter to the President of the Senate dated November 26th 1950, said that the money was to pay off old debts inherited from the Havana Electric Railway.[76] Details then emerged of previous business arrangements between Pawley and President Prío going back to September 1949.[77] William Pawley attempted to publicly defend his actions in front of a meeting of the Rotary Club of Havana and then in a subsequent newspaper article. *Bohemia*, an influential Havana weekly journal, described his speech as leaving members of the Rotary Club in a state of confusion and, reading a 20 page translated transcript produced by the US Embassy, one can see why.[78] Unravelling the figures from the self-justification indicates that the whole enterprise was to be financed by using one loan to pay the interest of another in a sort of pyramid deal.

At the end of October, Pawley had informed the British embassy of his intention to resign, claiming the President had not given him his support and was now refusing to see him. He also cited the problem of obstruction from labour leaders, blaming them for the fact that he could not get competent drivers, having to select them from ex-tram drivers. This resulted in a third of the 160 US buses being laid up due to accidents and lack of repairs. British diplomats seem inclined to take his word, describing the President as a "*sordid little Cuban politician*".[79] The British government was mainly concerned to ensure that the contract for Leyland buses continued and following a meeting in Leyland's offices it was agreed that the contract should not be cancelled if there was hope of receiving payment.[80]

The CIA would not have been surprised by Pawley's decision to resign, having had previous experience with him during the Second World War. Pawley had been one of the organisers of the "Flying Tigers", a squadron of US airmen, thinly disguised as volunteers, who had fought alongside the Chinese Nationalists against the Japanese invaders before the USA's formal entry into the hostilities. As the

---

76 *Bohemia* (10 December 1950) "En defensa de la ortodoxia y de Chibas" [Given the different stories that Pawley told to each of the interested parties, any similarity between amounts of money in any two letters must be seen as entirely coincidental]
77 *Bohemia* (6 July 1952) "Autobuses"
78   *Bohemia* (10 December 1950) "Pawley trata de defenderse"
    Bohemia (10 December 1950) "¿Que es más importante?"
    U.S. Embassy Havana, Despatch 1384 (3 January 1951)
79 FO 371/81476 - AK1372/10 (27 October 1950)*Omnibus Modernos of Havana*
80 FO 371/81476 - AK1372/12 (9 December 1950) *Leyland buses for Cuba*

June 1945 CIA report stated, he "*quit to increase his large personal income, left the American Volunteer Group at a critical time when they needed him most*".[81] This desertion also involved transferring the aircraft factory, which he was he was running in Rangoon to supply the Flying Tigers, to Bangalore in British controlled India.

This was not the first time the US intelligence agency had cause to doubt William Pawley. In 1942, they asked him to transport of secret documents to Cuba, but he put them in the open mail with the words "Secret and Confidential" on the outside. The Office of Censorship discovered that the letter had been steamed open before delivery.[82] It is impossible to say whether Pawley's intelligence operations, which seemed to be deeply intertwined with his business affairs, played a part in his activities in Cuba at this time. What is certain, however, is that he had friends in very high places and both British and Cuban officials made sure that, when *Autobuses Modernos* got in financial difficulty, Pawley did not lose any money.

As the financial problems of *Autobuses Modernos* became public knowledge, the Cuban government quickly moved in and nationalised the company to avoid further scandal.[83] The financial arrangements remained obscure, but a leaked report from the government-appointed administrator suggested losses of a quarter of a million pesos per month. It further appears that William Pawley had managed to get the buses registered as his personal property, leased from the Miami Railway Company, and that he then rented them to the company for 20 pesos a day each.[84] The British authorities still saw no reason to blame Pawley for the débâcle, rather blaming the other Havana bus company *Autobuses Aliados* who, the ECGD alleged, worked through labour elements in the government to provoke strikes and sabotage. They thought that the main problem lay with the fact that "*the President, upon whom Pawley had rested his faith, turned out to be a broken reed*". William Pawley's elaborate financial schemes might have worked if he had not been facing such a loose cannon as Marco Hirigoyen. His experiences with the unpredictable outcome of allowing gangsters and corrupt officials a free hand to implement Cold War anti-communism in the Cuban unions would have considerable knock-on effects later in the 1950s when he would be once again involved with the CIA. However, while the communists had been badly defeated on the buses, there would be a different story in the tobacco industry.

81 HSCA Segregated CIA Collection, Box 44, RIF#: 104-10122-10104 (11/09/59) CIA#: 80T01357A
82 HSCA Segregated CIA Collection, Box 44, RIF#: 104-10122-10104 (11/09/59) CIA#: 80T01357A
83 U.S. Embassy Havana, Despatch 1318 (21 December 1950)
84 *Bohemia* (17 December 1950) "Omnibus"

Tobacco

Cuban cigar exports had fallen from 256 million per year in 1906 to only 21 million in 1949.[85] Such was the obvious crisis that workers in the tobacco industry had accepted the argument for mechanisation for export, but were determined to resist mechanisation of the greatly expanded internal market, as well as demanding financial compensation for those displaced by machinery. However, the large employers were demanding mechanisation of the internal market in order to cover the costs of the new machinery. Moreover, they knew that this would displace the smaller producers from the internal market as they could not afford the cost of mechanisation. An extraordinary congress of the *Federación Tabacalera Nacional* (FTN, National Federation of Tobacco Workers) on 3rd and 4th October 1947 had accepted mechanisation for export but rejected it for the internal market. Within the context of their current struggle against mechanisation, tobacco workers gave considerable support to the *unitario* October 14th strike against the expulsion of Lázaro Peña from the *Palacio de los Trabajadores,* although many were arrested on their return to work.[86]

When Carlos Prío stood down as Minister of Labour in December 1947 in order to stand in the forthcoming presidential elections, Francisco Aguirre was appointed in his place as the reward for his work for the *Autenticos.* On 31st January 1948, Aquirre annulled the November 1946 FTN elections, but the *unitario* FTN took scant notice and on February 18th 1948 launched a campaign to defend hand rolling of cigars for domestic consumption at a mass meeting in the *Parque Central* in Havana, addressed by Lazaro Peña, who had been a tobacco worker and by Irma Montes de Oca, leader of the Havana *despalilladoras,* as the women who stripped the leaf from the tobacco stems were known. Aguirre appointed Manuel Campanería Rojas as the new head of the FTN and on April 1st Campanería organised an attack on the headquarters of the *Sindicato de Torcedores* (Cigar Rollers Union) in Central Havana, where Lazáro Peña and the displaced *unitario* leadership of the CTC had taken refuge. The attackers were repulsed by a large crowd of workers.[87] The next day, Campanería and 10 others attacked the *El Corona* cigar factory armed with pistols and killed Miguel Fernández Roig, union representative in the workshop, a popular leader of the Havana cigar makers; the gunmen escaped with the aid of the police.[88] On 23rd November 1948, while the Cuban parliament was discussing a motion which

85 Truslow, *Report on Cuba* (1951) pp.856-864
86 Duarte Hurtado, *La maquina torcedora de tabaco y las luchas en torno a su implementación en cuba* (1973) pp.117-149
87 *Hoy* (2 April 1948)
88 Stubbs, *Tobacco on the Periphery* (1985) p.153

would have legalised the complete mechanisation of cigar manufacture, further elections in the FTN resulted in an 88% victory for the *unitario* candidates led by Evelio Lugo.[89] The government replied with a police raid on the "*Sindicato de Torcedores*" in the early hours of Sunday 28th November and seized the building. The tobacco workers of Havana responded with a general strike during which over 900 pickets were arrested. The official CTC tried to persuade unemployed tobacco workers to take the jobs of the imprisoned strikers, but this move failed and the strike continued until everyone was released on the 30th. Work resumed the following day although a guerrilla war continued in the tobacco factories with frequent fights between workers and security guards.[90]

This campaign of violence was, however, only partially successful and the tobacco industry was one of the sectors where the PSP was to maintain a significant presence throughout the 1950s. Later attempts to intervene in the tobacco unions in Las Villas and Oriente in 1956 would be met with another series of strikes.[91]

Sugar

After the Allied victory in 1945, the US government began negotiations for a new trade agreement with the intention of reducing the cost of imported sugar. The *Federación Nacional de Trabajadores Azucareros* (FNTA - National Federation of Sugar Workers) sought the inclusion of organised labour in the official negotiating team, but President Grau initially refused and Jesús Menéndez, General Secretary of the FNTA went privately to Washington in an attempt to win US trade union support for the Cuban position. In the aftermath of these failed negotiations, the Cuban government withheld part of the 1946 sugar harvest and the US Secretary of Agriculture came to Havana for direct negotiations. This time, Jesús Menéndez was included in the official negotiating team and succeeded in inserting a Guarantee Clause in the final agreement which linked the price paid for sugar to inflation in goods imported from the USA. This resulted in a "*diferencial*" (differential) of thirty-six million pesos, from which the FNTA forced the government to distribute twenty-five million pesos amongst the sugar workers as a bonus (one peso was valued at one dollar during this period).[92]

---

89 *Hoy* (23, 24 November 1948)
90 *Hoy* (30 November, 1, 2 December 1948)
    Bohemia (5 December 1948) "¡Abran a la policía!"
    US Embassy, Airgram 1370 (30 November 1948)
91 *Carta Semanal* (15, 29 February, 21 March 1956)
92 Sims, *The Cuban Sugar Workers' Progress under the Leadership of a Black Communist, Jesús Menéndez Larrondo, 1941- 1948* (1993) pp.11-13

However, the following year, the US government was keen to cut the level of Cuban sugar imports from 5.7 to 3.2 million tons and thereby claw back some of the advantage that it had lost in the 1947 negotiations.[93] Jesús Menéndez visited Washington and New York in July 1947, campaigning for the retention of the 1946 level of imports and terms of purchase. He received the support of the Congress of Industrial Organizations (CIO), whose president Jacob Potovski succeeded in getting him an interview with the US Secretary of Agriculture, but to no avail as the Cuban Senate approved a new treaty on 25th July and President Grau annulled the Guarantee Clause with its *diferencial* bonus for sugar workers.[94]

Meanwhile, on April 30th 1947, Surí Castillo had set up an alternative FNTA. It only commanded a small minority of the membership, but Carlos Prío nevertheless recognised it as the official confederation. Despite the lack of official recognition, the *unitario* FNTA called a congress at the end of November 1947 which attracted an overwhelming majority of the local unions.[95] This congress decided to fight for a *diferencial* of 8% and the same wage levels as the previous year.[96] A campaign of strikes and demonstrations was organised from the beginning of the sugar harvest and the government responded by sending soldiers and the rural guard to intimidate and attack union meetings in the localities. Jesús Menéndez toured the eastern end of the island encouraging and supporting the strikes but, on January 22nd 1948, when he arrived at Matanzas station an army officer, Captain Joaquín Casillas, who claimed to be trying to arrest him despite his parliamentary immunity, shot him in the back and killed him.[97] It soon emerged that the order for the assassination was given by the Chief of the Army General Staff.[98] Menéndez's funeral in Havana was attended by 150,000 people and there were a large number of protest strikes. Mere protest, however would prove insufficient to deter the government and the mujalistas from their murderous campaign.

However, the *unitarios* had not, as yet, evolved any strategy to deal with the death squads. Carlos Prío introduced an anti-gangster law early in his presidency. The effect of this law was negligible in its effects on the activities of the gangs themselves, but it ensured that any attempt by militant workers or Communists to

---

93 *New York Herald Tribune* (27 July 1947) "Keep Cuba a Good Customer by Raising the Sugar Quota"
    Hoy, (16 July 1947)
94 Hoy, (18, 23 July 1947)
    Revista Azúcar, (June 1947) p. 4
95 Hoy (16-20 November 1947)
96 Hoy (23 November 1947)
97 García Galló, *General de las cañas* (1998) pp.158-153
98 FO 371/67970 - AN0684 (20 February 1948) *Assassination of Cuban Communist*

arm themselves in self-defence could be ruthlessly suppressed in the name of the fight against crime. The anti-Communist gangs had official support and police protection and any armed groups of workers would have faced the full repressive force of the state. However, the fact that *Hoy* felt the need to firmly but patiently explain the problems with small armed groups is an indication that there was rank and file pressure for such a response.[99] The struggle to defend sugar workers' pay and conditions continued under the leadership of another Communist, Ursinio Rojas and it would be this more generalised class struggle that would start to offer a mass response to the wave of murders. Nevertheless, the murder of Jesús Menéndez was a severe blow to the Cuban labour movement and there would be several more such blows.

The Port of Havana

In 1938, Aracelio Iglesias was elected Secretary of the *Sindicato de Estibadores y Jornaleros de la Bahia de La Habana* (Union of Stevedores and Labourers of the Bay of Havana) and in 1939 to the National Executive of the *Federación Obrera Maritima Nacional* (FOMN, National Maritime Workers' Federation) as well as the National Executive of the CTC. He also represented the FOMN on the *Comisión de Inteligencia del Puerto* (Port Arbitration Committee) which set the rates for loading and unloading ships. There was no enforcement mechanism for arbitration decisions and he did not hesitate to call strikes and boycotts against any company slow to comply. He also successfully negotiated with the Ministry of Labour to establish a strict rota system for employment in the port of Havana.

The Second World War was a period of high inflation in Cuba, but the Havana FOMN was able to put sufficient pressure on the government to decree wage increases which went some way to keeping pace with this inflation. Iglesias's uncompromising stance on this and other demands earned him the enmity the US War Shipping Administration which, on behalf of the major US shipping lines, was using the wartime emergency to attack established wages and conditions of work.[100] The end of the Second World War saw an increased level of industrial disputes in the face of the employers' attempts to increase productivity. In particular there was constant conflict over the introduction of bulk loading of sugar, as well as the freight ferry links to Florida known as the Sea-Train.[101] Aracelio Iglesias was the Bob Crow of his day and the pro-business press directed

---

99 *Hoy* (23 September 1949)
100 Canton Navarro, *Aracelio Iglesias* (1977) p.23
101 Partido Comunista De Cuba (PCC), *Historia del movimiento obrero cubano, tomo II* (1985) pp.208-210

considerable animosity towards him as the public face of the Havana dockers.[102] US Senator Bradley, spokesman for the shipping lines, called him the "*Red Czar of the Port of Havana*" and claimed that he was responsible for the highest wages paid to stevedores anywhere in the world.[103]

In February 1948, the Ministry of Labour imposed Gilberto Goliath and Juán Arévalo as leaders of the FOMN and the Communist daily *Hoy*, reminded its readers of Arévalo's links with Serafino Romualdi and the AFL, whose hand they saw behind this particular move.[104] In Santiago de Cuba, the stevedore Juan Taquechel, Secretary General of the *Federación General de Trabajadores de Oriente* (FGTO General Federation of Workers in Oriente Province), was also removed from his post by police on the instruction of the Ministry of Labour in the same month. Aracelio Iglesias had a sufficient base of support to be re-elected FOMN secretary for the port of Havana by a mass meeting in March 1948.[105] The government annulled the election and the Navy, Maritime Police and soldiers forced their way onto the dock, occupied the FOMN hiring hall and gave formal control of the union to supporters of the CON(A).[106] This led to strikes and demonstrations which made it evident that the Havana dockers would not easily accept the imposed leadership. On 15th October 1948, a mass meeting organized by Aracelio Iglesias voted to refuse to pay their union subscriptions and two days later he was murdered, shot in the back by two gunmen.[107] Strikes broke out throughout the country in the days that followed and his funeral became a massive protest in itself.

On 28th September 1949, Emilio Surí Castillo, now general secretary of the official sugar workers federation, called at the US Embassy in Havana, accompanied by his secretary along with a man called Julio Oropesa who, the report of the meeting said, "*runs race horses*", a euphemism for a gangster involved in the corrupt gambling associated with the Havana race course. They informed the Second Secretary, John Cope, that they had assisted the recent escape from prison of a gangster named Soler.[108] John Cope informed the Secretary of State that "*Soler had deliberately killed Iglesias at the instance of the Suri Castillo faction*". The visitors went on to say that "*the Communists are still powerful*

---

102 *Bohemia* (16 March 1947) "La congestión de los muelles habaneros"
103 Canton Navarro, *Aracelio Iglesias* (1977) p.25
104 *Hoy* (5 February 1948)
105 *Hoy* (16 March 1948)
106 *Hoy* (18 April 1948)
107 *Bohemia* (24 October 1948) "El no.1 de la cordialidad"
108 John Cope has confused Rafael Soler, who was the actual murderer of Aracelio Iglesias, with Policarpo Soler another, equally violent gangster who had also recently escaped from police custody.

amongst the dock workers and it is necessary to eliminate two more leaders in order for the non-Communist faction to gain control". They added that there were "*about 12 more Communist leaders that must be eliminated as soon as possible*". The Embassy Second Secretary politely declined the visitors' request to assist with arms shipments from Miami, but said that visa requests for any of Surí's lieutenants who found it necessary to flee Cuba should be "*presented in the proper manner*".[109] There is nothing in the memorandum which indicates that the Embassy official found anything unusual in discussing the murder of trade union officials and the escape of the perpetrators.

The murder of Aracelio Iglesias was a serious setback for the workers in the port of Havana, but their organization was strong enough to continue resisting productivity measures such that, in 1959 at the victory of the Cuban Revolution, bulk loading of sugar had still not been introduced and the plan for the Sea-Train had long since been abandoned.

Camagüey

While we have so far concentrated on the situation in Havana, there is a large collection of documents in the Provincial Archive in the city of Camagüey in central Cuba which shed light on the implementation of the purges outside the capital. These illustrate the way in which the government was able to use respect for the law to purge the print-workers' union, *Sindicato de Artes Gráficas* (Graphic Arts Union).

In 1942, the leader of the Camagüey printers was a Communist called Manuel Padrero.[110] Following the election victory of Ramon Grau San Martín in 1944, the agreement at national level to share control with the *Autenticos* resulted in Rafael de la Torre becoming treasurer (*Secretario de Financias*). Clearly this was not a successful working arrangement as there were a series of resignations and new elections which left Manuel Padrero as General Secretary in October 1945.[111] The situation worsened to the extent that the returning officer for the January 1946 elections wrote to the local police captain to ask for the presence of a police officer to maintain order at the election meeting. Manuel Padrero emerged from this skirmish as General Secretary of the *Sindicato* but in the next election in December 1946, he lost his attempt to become organising secretary by 19 votes to

---

109 US Embassy Havana, Dispach 757 (3 October 1949) *Further Indications of Growing Hostility Between Communist and Non-Communist Factions in Cuba*

110 Archivo Provincial de Camagüey, Fondo Movimiento Obrero, Expediente 100, Legajo 3

111 Archivo Provincial de Camagüey, Fondo Movimiento Obrero, Expediente 101, 102, Legajo 3

29, while Rafael de la Torre was elected General Secretary.[112] Padrero then wrote to the local head of the Ministry of Labour complaining about the procedures and a new general meeting was ordered, which voted 36-3 to endorse the previous elections and to give immediate control to Rafael de la Torre.[113]

Two factors seem of importance here. Firstly that Padrero considers that it is perfectly acceptable to involve the Ministry in the internal affairs of the union when he loses an election, citing a minor irregularity but not suggesting real corruption. This is clearly a case of him being a "bad loser", because he then suffers a crushing defeat in the subsequent meeting. Secondly, we know this whole story through the extensive paperwork that the union provided to the Ministry of Labour: minutes of the meetings in a rigidly proscribed format, listing those present at the meetings, affidavits as to accuracy and general information that trade unionists in most of the rest of the world would consider to be confidential union business.

That the end of 1946 was a particularly turbulent time in the trade union movement in Camagüey can also be seen from a circular from the *Federación de Trabajadores de la Provincia de Camagüey* (Workers' Federation of the Province of Camagüey), the provincial body representing all affiliates to the CTC. This condemns the local Ministry official for changing the rules for elections in a manner not authorised by decree 1026. The circular urges that telegrams be sent to the Ministry of Labour and to the president of the Republic. However, other documents indicate that the leadership of the *Federación de Trabajadores de la Provincia de Camagüey* were much more militant and had a more secure base than those who ran the printers' union. Nevertheless, they still seemed to accept such gross interference in the internal affairs of the union as normal. If Cuban trade unionists were used to such close supervision by the Ministry of Labour, sending telegrams of protest when dissatisfied, but not taking more serious defensive action, then they would be unprepared for a surprise "intervention".

However, Julian Sotolongo, a sugar worker and *unitario* leader of the *Federación de Trabajadores de la Provincia de Camagüey* seems to have been made of sterner stuff than his comrades in the printers' union. Recovering quickly from the attack on his local federation by the head of the local office of the Ministry of Labour, he condemned the expulsion from the *Palacio de los Trabajadores* in a 10 page speech blaming the American Federation of Labor and

112 Archivo Provincial de Camagüey, Fondo Movimiento Obrero, Expediente 107, Legajo 3
113 Archivo Provincial de Camagüey, Fondo Movimiento Obrero, Expediente 108, 109, Legajo 3

speaking of the short protest strikes.[114] He managed to win the elections in December 1948 and was recognised as such by the Ministry.[115] In January 1949 he called a meeting of all affiliated unions to discuss the immediate tasks of the *unitario* movement and in April of that year issued a leaflet calling for a united May Day march to oppose bulk-loading of sugar and to apply the decisions of the recently held Sixth Congress of the CTC (*unitario*). Supporters of the official CTC were encouraged to attend, although he referred to them under the rather insulting name of *cetekeros*.[116] This was probably too much for the Ministry as thereafter Sotolongo's leaflets were issued in the name of "*Acción Sindical Unitaria*" (United Union Action) rather than the official *Federación de Trabajadores de la Provincia de Camagüey*, although details of exactly how and when the purges happened in Camagüey are not to be found in the archives.[117] What is clear is that many of these *unitario* militants managed to continue operating in one form or another - particularly in the docks and sugar industry.

A 1951 leaflet from the *Comité Ejecutivo del Sindicato de Trabajadores Azucareros del Central Vertientes* (Executive Committees of the Union of Sugar Workers in Central Vertientes, situated some 30km south west of Camagüey city) calls for the *divisionistas* (splitters) to be unmasked as being more interested in money than the welfare of their fellow union members. It complains that they were robbed of the *diferencial* in 1948, had unelected leaders forced upon them, while they had been democratically elected, and called for a 30% wage increase or no *zafra* (sugar harvest) in 1952.[118] The Camagüey archive also contains a leaflet addressed to the sugar workers of *Central Estrella* in Camagüey province.[119] The workers at *Central Estrella* went on strike in February 1955 against a large number of redundancies, led by a semi-clandestine *Comité de Lucha* (Struggle Committee). This was an unofficial body which was made up of the previous local union leadership who had been removed by government intervention; such bodies, under a variety of names, appeared and disappeared in many strike situations, but were created to give organisational form to militant workers who had been purged from the official structures. The *Central Estrella* workers were able to wage a fundamentally successful strike, which forced the employers to negotiate with the deposed workers' representatives and reinstate the sacked workers. Their success

---

114 Archivo Provincial de Camagüey, Fondo Movimiento Obrero, Expediente 33, Legajo 1
115 Archivo Provincial de Camagüey, Fondo Movimiento Obrero, Expediente 15, Legajo 1
116 *cetekeros* is Spanish expression meaning those who support the CTK
    Archivo Provincial de Camagüey, Fondo Movimiento Obrero, Expediente 17, Legajo 1
117 Archivo Provincial de Camagüey, Fondo Movimiento Obrero, Expediente 128, Legajo 4
118 Archivo Provincial de Camagüey, Fondo Movimiento Obrero, Expediente 58, Legajo 2
119 Archivo Provincial de Camagüey, Fondo Movimiento Obrero, Expediente 57, Legajo 2

showed that being deprived of control of the official trade union machinery did not necessarily mean the end of their ability to resist, provided of course that there were militants willing to take risks and lead effective unofficial action.[120] As was so often the case, the dockers provide the best example of such action.

A surviving leaflet in the Camagüey archive in the name of the *Sindicato del Puerto de Guyabel* (Union of the Port of Guyabel, on the south coast of Camagüey province) speaks of the problem of the new maritime terminal proposed by the Francisco Sugar Company. The government had authorised the construction of new port facilities and the company was conducting a propaganda campaign against the union. The leaflet asks rhetorically "What are we opposed to then?" They raised three objections:

- Against the 87 job losses the construction of the port would entail;

- Against bulk loading of sugar;

- Opposed to sugar currently being embarked at the ports of Nuevitas and Santa Cruz being diverted to the new port for bulk loading.

They are insistent that they will not sign a new agreement without these problems being resolved. The murder of Arecelio Iglesias clearly did not intimidate these *unitario* port workers.

Nevertheless, such continued militancy had its dangers. On 18th September 1949, in *Central Francisco* in Camagüey province, Surí Castillo arranged for the summoning of a general meeting of the sugar workers' union to discuss threatened wage cuts. A Communist, Amancio Rodríguez, who had been removed from his previous leadership position during the purges, attended the meeting along with a group of *unitario* militants with the intention of intervening. As soon as they tried to speak, Oscar Fáez, who had been appointed to run the local union by Surí, drew his pistol and fatally shot one of the *unitarios*, another Communist called José Oviedo. A group of five gunmen then opened fire on the *unitario* group, killing Amancio Rodríguez and wounding three others. The gunmen were apprehended by a crowd of angry sugar workers as they attempted to escape in a private aeroplane owned by Emilio Surí Castillo.[121]

Sixth Congress

Amancio Rodríguez and José Oviedo were killed attempting to implement the

120 Pérez Pérez, *La huelga de 55 en el Central Estrella* (1974)
121 *Hoy* (20 September 1949)

decisions of the Sixth Congress of the *unitario* CTC. By early 1949 it was becoming obvious that the support of the government for the official CTC meant that the *unitarios* had to adopt new tactics. The old leadership still had considerable support amongst organised workers, as photographs of the 1949 May Day parades indicate; the numbers attending the *unitario* events vastly outnumbered those at the official function.[122] The *unitario* CTC convened a Sixth Congress which started on 8th April 1949 chaired by Ursinio Rojas, who had taken over as sugar workers' leader following the murder of Jesús Menéndez. In his General Secretary's report Lázaro Peña discussed various errors that they had made since the 1947 split. He said that they had concentrated on securing subscriptions from workers to the neglect of a political struggle with the reformists who controlled the official CTC apparatus and had abandoned local unions that came under CON(A) leadership. As a result, he admitted, the CTC had lost contact with large numbers of workers. To correct this, he proposed that, where appropriate, *unitarios* should go back into the "CTK" local unions, set up *Comités de Lucha y Unidad* (Committees for Unity and Struggle) and attempt to organise united action against intensification of workloads and for improved wages and conditions. The final resolution of the congress called for "direct mobilisation of the masses" and the development of joint action between *unitarios* and the "CTK" rank and file.[123]

This new approach was, in fact, an attempt to spread tactics already developing in some of the more militant workplaces; the dockers in Havana had set up a committee to oppose the Sea-Train and Communist railway workers had organised a *Comité Pro-Unidad Ferroviario* (Railway Unity Committee).[124] The Communist bus workers had already returned to activity and full membership of the transport workers' union, despite it still being dominated by the gangsters of *Acción Revolucionaria Guiteras* (ARG). There were, of course, difficulties to be overcome. Many workers had abandoned the trade union movement altogether, the union bureaucracy placed many obstacles in the way of those individuals or local unions wishing to rejoin and the violence was ongoing. Moreover, many *unitario* militants were unconvinced of the need to change, seeing those of their colleagues who had joined the "CTK" as little short of blacklegs.[125] Above all, trade unions are large, unwieldy organisations with a tendency to bureaucracy, making the implementation of changes of political line very slow to take effect.

---

122 *Hoy* (3 May 1949)
123 *Hoy* (10, 17 April 1949)
124 *Hoy* (10, 11 March, 3 April 1949)
125 PCC, *Historia del movimiento obrero cubano, tomo II* (1985) p.233

Many historians with little understanding of the nature of workplace organisation see the PSP and the "Communist" CTC as monolithic and obedient to the decisions of the leadership. In reality there were political and personal differences within both organisations which gave rise to considerable debate and final decisions were implemented with more or less enthusiasm according to the personal and political priorities of the persons concerned. The PSP had been a minority group amongst the leadership of the CTC before the split and there were still a significant number of *Autentico* workers who remained loyal to Lazaro Peña for a variety of reasons: respect for a local or national leader, disgust with the murders and corruption of the official CTC, even simply force of habit. To these can be added the *Sección Obrera* (Workers section) of the *Ortodoxos,* which was home to a considerable number of militants who did not agree with the PSP, but who hated the CON(A) for its corruption. Finally, workplace solidarity frequently trumps outside political affiliations and it is common for working class activists to feel more loyalty to their work colleagues than to their formal political affiliation. This meant that there would be a period of intense debate and argument before the policy was fully implemented but, by the beginning of 1951, most of the *unitario* federations had disbanded, withered away or managed to return to the officially recognised federation. Given that the active membership of the *unitario* CTC, as well as the unofficial committees and networks of militants which replaced it, spread much wider than the ranks of the PSP and encompassed a wide range of political opinion, the use of the term "*unitario*" rather than "Communist" for this movement seems perfectly justified.

The tactical change began by setting up *Comités Pro-Primero de Mayo* (May Day committees); we have already seen how Julian Sotolongo put this into practice in Camagüey.[126] A tactic of "unity in action" requires an action to unite around and *unitario* activists set about fomenting small scale disputes; an example of this approach was the strike at *Delicia y Chaparra* sugar mill in March 1949. Local *unitario* militants led an unofficial walkout over work intensification and the police replied with over 700 arrests. The complete plantation complex, owned by the Cuban-American Sugar Company, was paralysed for 5 days. Then the FNTA bureaucracy in Havana negotiated a settlement with the Ministry of Labour and Surí proposed that this "harmonious solution" should be accepted and ordered a return to work. This caused enough of a split in the strikers' ranks to break the strike.[127] An examination of this and many other similar industrial disputes at the

126 Archivo Provincial de Camagüey, Fondo Movimiento Obrero, Expediente 17, Legajo 1
127 *Hoy* (12, 13, 17, 18, 20 March 1949)

time show that the *unitarios* frequently had sufficient strength to call unofficial strikes, but did not have enough influence to prevent the Havana-based trade union bureaucracy selling them out. Nevertheless, this was a sound basis on which to build a network of militants capable of intervening in the industrial struggle.

Undermining CTAL

Eusebio Mujal himself was now ready for the next stage of his intervention in the CTC. By 1949, Angel Cofiño had served his purpose. In the 1947 split, his notionally independent position had given cover to the CON(A) conspirators as he had a genuine base in the electrical workers' federation, having been legitimately elected as General Secretary of the electrical workers' federation. His position as CTC General Secretary was precarious and he was isolated on the national executive, surrounded by *Auténticos* who did their best to undermine him. Another reason he had to go was his unpopularity with Romualdi and the AFL because he was sympathetic to the Peronist Argentine trade union confederation and was not considered to be sufficiently opposed to the CTAL; he had prevented a motion to disaffiliate from CTAL being moved at the conference in 1947 when he was elected to lead the breakaway CTC.[128] While he was in hospital in March 1949, Francisco Aguirre, now deputy General Secretary of the official CTC, convened a *Consejo Nacional* (National Council) which forced Cofiño's resignation, appointed Francisco Aguirre as interim General Secretary and convened a Sixth Congress for 27th to 29th April.[129] Aguirre clearly hoped to be elected General Secretary, but was outmanoeuvred by Eusabio Mujal who reached an agreement with the ARG and was himself elected as General Secretary of the CTC with Surí Castillo as his deputy. Once he had secured control of the CTC, Eusebio Mujal ruthlessly dominated the confederation with the help of the Ministry of Labour and the police where necessary. He rewarded his friends with lucrative positions and kick-backs, while destroying the career of anyone who got in his way.[130] His name became a by-word for corruption and such was his dominance that the adjective *mujalista* became universally applied to the official CTC. Cofiño took his own electrical workers and their allies in the telephone workers' federation out of the CTC to form a new organisation the *Confederación General de Trabajo* (CGT - General Confederation of Labour) but it did not last long and they returned to the CTC fairly quickly.[131] We therefore see that, at least in formal, organisational terms, the

128 LAB 13/545 (1 June 1949) *State of the Cuban Labour Movement*
129 FO 371/73994 - AN 1556 (10 May 1949) *6th CTC congress*
130 Rojas Blaquier, *El mujalismo en el movimiento obrero cubano* (1983)
131 LAB 13/545 (10 May 1949) *6th CTC Congress* & (1 June 1949) *State of the Cuban Labour Movement*

plans hatched initially by Juan Arévalo and Serafino Romualdi to split the CTC and to place anti-Communists in control of the officially recognised bureaucracy had borne fruit, although not quite in the way Arévalo had envisaged; he was murdered by gangsters on 1st September 1948, probably on the instructions of Emilio Surí Castillo who saw him as being too honest.[132]

The Cold War in Europe and the USA started in the middle of 1947; US Secretary of State George Marshall announced the European Recovery Program (Marshall Plan) on 5th June, the *US Labor Management Relations Act (Taft-Hartley)* was enacted on 23rd June and the CIA was formed on 18th September. In this context, Serafino Romualdi's April 1947 article entitled *Labor and Democracy in Latin America* can be seen as the formal declaration of the Cold War within the wider Latin American labour movement.[133] The events surrounding the split in the CTC indicate that the Cold War started particularly early in Cuba and was not initiated by the US State Department, which does not appear to have intervened directly, although there was a general awareness of the US government's approval of the anti-Communist interventions.[134] In these early stages, the main focus of the US anti-Communist trade union activity was in Europe, in particular funding the split in the French CGT and the Italian CGIL, while the principal figures in the newly elected president Truman's administration knew little of Latin America. The European focus of the official Cold War left Romualdi and the AFL a free hand to operate in Latin America.

The takeover of the Cuban CTC by anti-Communists gave Romualdi a base from which to organise against Lombardo and the CTAL. In January 1948, the AFL and the Cuban CTC were the main players in setting up the *Confederación Interamericana de Trabajadores* (CIT - Interamerican Confederation of Workers) with Romualdi as Secretary. Its headquarters moved to Havana the following year and Francisco Aguirre, no longer Minister of Labour and back in charge of the restaurant workers' federation, became its secretary, probably as a consolation prize for being denied the main job of General Secretary of the CTC.[135] In 1951, the CIT changed its name to the *Organización Regional Interamericana de Trabajadores* (ORIT - Interamerican Regional Organisation of Workers) with

---

U.S. Embassy Havana, Despatch 2099, (1951) *Labor Developments in Cuba 1950*
PCC, *Historia del movimiento obrero cubano, tomo II* (1985) pp.216-219
132 FO 371/67972 - AN 3376 (3 September 1948) *Murder of Juan Arévalo*
   Bohemia (21 January 1951)
133 Romualdi, *Labor and Democracy in Latin America* (1947)
134 Bethell & Roxborough, *Postwar conjuncture in Latin America* (1992) p.26
135 FO 371/74725 (7 September 1949) *Advance report on proceedings of the Inter-American Confederation of Workers*

Aguirre still General Secretary.[136] However, Aguirre proved to be too corrupt, incompetent and lazy and the corruption in the Cuban CTC was making it an embarrassing liability. He was forced out in February 1952, having served his purpose, and was replaced by, Luis Alberto Monge from Costa Rica, under whose leadership, ORIT managed to completely outmanoeuvre Lombardo and the CTAL, effectively replacing it by the mid-1950s. Thus, in terms of international Cold War politics, the AFL collaboration with anti-Communist Cuban trade unionists was successful. In the specifically Cuban context however, it was less so as an upturn in the class struggle in 1950 started to escape the control of the CTC bureaucracy.

Strikes

The area where the *mujalista* takeover had been least successful was the tobacco industry. Despite formal control of the FTN (*Federación Tabacalera Nacional* - National Federation of Tobacco Workers) passing to Manuel Campanería Rojas, who had murdered Manuel Roig in the attack on the *La Corona* workshop, the deposed *unitario* general secretary Evelio Lugo, was still the effective leader of the tobacco workers. In August 1949, faced with a proposed law to mechanise the production of cigars for domestic consumption, Lugo met with representatives of the smaller producers whose livelihoods were threatened by mechanisation. Between August 1949 and March 1950, joint committees of workers and smaller employers were set up to campaign against the proposal to mechanise the home market. The campaign was launched by a strike on 27th March and demonstrations outside a number of town halls were followed by some large demonstrations in Havana, despite police bans and other repressive actions. In response to police violence, in July 1951 there was a successful call in the main tobacco producing towns for *ciudades muertas* ("dead cities", a form of town-wide general strike that also involved businesses closing voluntarily). The tension was greatly exacerbated when the police shot dead a protester, Alfredo López Brito, in Cabaiguán and the townsfolk started to arm themselves. Seeing that they were in danger of losing control of the situation, the government withdrew the decree and there was no further mention of mechanisation for the home market.[137] Throughout this campaign, the leaders of the official CTC were effectively marginalised and small scale gangster violence was shown to be useless. Even the state forces of repression proved inadequate to deal with the mass protests and the government and big business suffered a considerable setback.

---

136 FO 371/90461 (January 1951) *Inter-American Congress of the International Confederation of Free Trade Unions, Mexico City*
137 Stubbs, *Tobacco on the Periphery* (1985) pp.154-156

January 1950 also saw strikes in various sugar *centrales* in Camagüey, Las Villas, Pinar del Rio and Havana provinces, as well as a strike on the Matanzas docks. The sugar workers took action to defend the right to 48 hours pay for 44 hours work. Julian Sotolongo, still using the title Secretary General of the *Federación de Trabajadores de Camagüey* (Labour Federation of Camagüey), called a meeting in solidarity with the workers in the *Central Francisco*, where it will be recalled the *unitario* leaders had been murdered the previous year, and succeeded in instigating a number of solidarity strikes. Despite this, the movement in *Central Francisco* was defeated when the army moved in and broke the strike. This wave of strikes culminated in a 24 hour general strike in the city of Matanzas in protest at the threat to move sugar exports to other ports. The fact that the local military commander was the same Captain Joaquín Casillas who had murdered Jesús Menéndez only added fuel to the flames. The results of these strikes in the sugar industry were mixed, in some places, direct negotiations between the employers and local *unitario* leaders produced some successful results, in others the army and police used violence to force a return to work.[138]

There were more strikes in the sugar industry at the end of March and the beginning of April 1950, this time over work intensification. The economist Jacinto Torres, chief economist of the CTC, estimated that the rhythm of production had increased 41% between 1942 and 1949. This provoked the demand for payment of "*superproduccion*" (overproduction), that is compensation for the loss of earning due to productivity increases. The US Embassy estimated that 95% of the sugar mills went on strike, starting on 29th March. Again, while many employers settled with their workers locally, this time, however, the government also decreed the payment of a bonus of 6 days pay to all sugar workers on 12th April, although Surí Castillo did manage to seize, in the name of arrears of union subscriptions, a day's pay from the bonus before it was paid. Despite this government decree being accepted by the official FNTA, while the army and police continued to violently attack mass meetings and arrest strikers, the strike wave did not finally peter out until the 20th, with many groups of workers securing better local agreements.[139] The strike movement caught the union bureaucracy by surprise and they had to run to catch up with this strike wave which covered six provinces. And meanwhile, even though the FOMN bureaucracy accepted an agreement with the port employers, dockers went on

---

138 *Hoy* (21, 22, 23, 24, 25, 26, 28, 29 January 1950)
    U.S. Embassy Havana, Despatch 212 (31 January, 1950) *Labor Notes on Havana, Jan. 11-30, 1950*
139 U.S. Embassy Havana, Despatch 193 (26 July, 1950) *Labor Developments in Cuba--Second Quarter 1950*
    Hoy (28, 29, 31 March, 1, 4, 5, 6, 7, 11, 12, 13, 15, 18, 19, 20 April)

strike in half a dozen ports scattered across the island.[140] The government had to pay $100,000 to stevedores in ten ports to finally settle the issue.[141]

The sugar strikes broke out simultaneously across a number of provinces; this could only have happened if there was an effective network of militants able to generalise and plan such action. A new leadership was emerging following the murders; most noticeable amongst these are the sugar workers Ursinio Rojas and Julian Sotolongo as well as the dock workers Pablo Sandoval and Juán Taquechel. The PSP had renounced Browderism in 1946 and the killings of such prominent trade unionists had made it quite clear that there was no way back to respectability for the Cuban Communists but, if there was any doubt, the government turned its attention directly to undermining the PSP. On 24th August 1950, the government sent police to seize the office and printing works of *Hoy*.[142] The Communist newspaper was silenced until the end of August the following year when the courts ruled that the government intervention was illegal.[143] This court decision produced an outburst of officially instigated gangsterism, the *Hoy* printing presses were badly damaged by a masked gang on 24th September and an attempt was made on the life of the newspaper's director, Anibal Escalante, on 17th October.[144] In the changed circumstances, those who wanted to fight started to come to the fore, while the faint hearted and opportunists went over to Mujal or just fled.

However, this strike wave did mark the end of gangster attacks on individual trade unionists. Once industrial action reached a certain critical mass, small groups of gangsters were of no use to the government, even the army, police and rural guard were stretched too thin. Meanwhile the trade union bureaucracy became impotent as employers had no alternative but to negotiate with local leaders, whether they were officially recognised or not, and the *mujalistas* struggled to regain control. Moreover, once in control of the unions and retirement funds, there was no further need to murder workers' leaders, indeed there was the danger that to continue would be counterproductive. However, as the gangs turned their attention away from killing trade unionists, they showed an increasing tendency to turn their guns on each other as they disputed the spoils. Billed as an agreement to end the

---

140 U.S. Embassy Havana, Despatch 193 (26 July, 1950) *Labor Developments in Cuba--Second Quarter 1950*
    Hoy (15, 18, 19, 20, 21, 22 April)
141 U.S. Embassy Havana, Despatch 264 (3 August, 1950) *Labor* Notes-Habana-July 1950
142 *Bohemia* (3 September 1950)
    U.S. Embassy Havana, Despatch 455 (28 August, 1950) *Cuban Government Intervenes Communist Newspaper*
143 U.S. Embassy Havana, Despatch 369 (30 August, 1951) *Reappearance of Communist Newspaper Hoy*
144 U.S. Embassy Havana, Despatch 539 (28 September, 1951) *Hoy Presses Damaged by Masked Gang*
    U.S. Embassy Havana, Despatch 654 (19 October, 1951) *Anibal Escalante assassination attempt*
    Hoy (17 October 1951)
    Bohemia (21 October 1951)

bloodshed, the government brokered the so-called "Pact of the Groups" in May 1951 whereby the gangs agreed to "bury their old hatreds and dedicate themselves to constructive political and social activities".[145] Many observers saw this as the final act in the establishment of Prío's gangster kleptocracy, given that it would allow prominent *pistoleros* to run for elective office and thereby profit from parliamentary immunity. Lesser gunmen were given jobs in the state bureaucracy. The *Ortodoxo* newspaper *Alerta* charged that 2,120 sinecures in the public service were distributed among the groups with additional payments totalling $18,000 a month being made to the gangs directly from the presidential palace.[146] And as often happens when politicians use gangsters they think they can control, the gangsters ended up controlling the politicians. An example of this is the case of Policarpo Soler, a well-known gunman, who had left Havana following a suggestion from the Secretary of the Council of Ministers that this would "avoid problems". He went to Matanzas where he started preparing to run for public office, but had not relinquished his old ways and was arrested after murdering two rivals. He was held in Matanzas prison "like an honoured guest" from where he spoke to the press of "sensational revelations".[147] He was transferred to Havana to the *Castillo del Principe* prison, from where he "escaped" on 25th November in circumstances which left no doubt that there had been official connivance.[148] Similarly, the *mujalista* bureaucracy had developed interests of its own and they used their knowledge of the Prio government's involvement in their murderous and corrupt rise to control of the CTC in order to blackmail him into meeting their demands, among which were wage rises and job protection for union members to help secure their base. This was not quite what the AFL had in mind when they started interfering in Cuban union politics.

Regime in Crisis

Serafino Romualdi explains in his autobiography that the role of ORIT was not just political anti-communism, but also to create:

> *a new type of Latin American trade union leader who, abandoning the customary concept of the class struggle, would substitute constructive relations between the workers and the employers.[149]*

Removing Communists from office in the trade unions for international

---

145 *Bohemia* (13 May 1951) cited in Ameringer, *The Cuban Democtaric Experience* (2000) pp.151-2
146 *Alerta* (4 March 1951)
147 *Bohemia* (24 June 1951)
148 *Bohemia* (2 December 1951)
149 Romualdi, *Presidents and Peons* (1967) p.5

political reasons was only part of the rationale behind the Cold War; increasing productivity and raising profit levels were equally important.[150] The persistent interventions and frequent murders had broadly achieved the anti-Communist political objective but failed to restrict workers' demands, as shown by the report on the state of the Cuban economy prepared for the International Bank for Reconstruction and Development (World Bank) in 1951, which bewailed the high wages and staffing levels.[151] This was because, in order to maintain some semblance of legitimacy, the *mujalista* bureaucracy of the CTC had to produce economic gains for their membership and, much to the annoyance of the employers, they combined this with corrupt demands for personal bribes to settle disputes. From the employers' point of view, at least the Communists had been honest. Now the employers had difficulty working out with whom to negotiate if there was a strike. The *mujalistas* normally, despite their bluster, did not initiate real industrial action so, while frequently demanding bribes to call off action, they were frequently unable to restore normal working. On the other hand, the real organisers of the strikes, the often unknown *unitario* militants who had stayed the course, were now embittered after seeing their comrades murdered, their unions stolen and were thus in no mood to compromise. The reports from the British Embassy are full of references to the *"endless irresponsible demands of labour"*[152], while the *Asociación Nacional de Industriales de Cuba* (ANIC - National Association of Industrialists) issued a statement charging the government with blocking economic progress by its demagogic policy of making unreasonable demands on employers and failing to comply with labour contracts. In particular, they said, it was it difficult to attract US capital in order to expand industry in Cuba.[153]

Despite being able to secure higher wage increases than the employers thought justified, the *mujalista* trade union bureaucracy was clearly not held in any great affection by the rank and file workers. The British Embassy reports the strong provincial organisation established by the *unitarios* had been destroyed as part of the takeover of the CTC and the bureaucracy was left without an efficient means of collecting subscriptions. This was not a great problem at first as they received a state subsidy, but a more permanent solution was required.[154] The solution agreed with the government was for compulsory check-off of union dues. The decree

150 Carew, *Labour Under the Marshall Plan* (1987)
151 Truslow, *Report on Cuba* (1951)
152 FO 371/97515 - AK1011/1 (14 January 1952) *Annual review of Cuba for 1951*
    Diario de la Marina quoted in *Havana Post* (16 March 1952)
153 U.S. Embassy Havana, Despatch 570 (3 October 1951) *Summary of Labor Developments During First Half of 1951*
154 LAB 13/545 (April 1950) *Labour situation Nov 1949 - Apr 1950*

establishing this was unpopular with employers and workers alike, with the PSP making much of it in their propaganda and the employers fighting it through the courts. In April 1951, a presidential decree established the measure, initially in the sugar industry, and obliged the employer to pay 1% of their wage bill to the FNTA and the CTC. Many workers threatened to strike if the deduction was made to their wages and in many cases this meant that the employers had to pay the union subscription from their own profits.[155] Most business owners thought that this just added insult to injury.

But it was not just big business that was alienated. By the end of 1951, the Prío government was widely despised among most sections of society because of its corruption and criminal associations. However, the government managed to produce its own crisis by increasing fares on public transport from 5¢ to 8¢. Public transport in Havana was a shambles, made worse by the domination of the trade union by the gangsters of the ARG. To increase the fares in these circumstances caused a public outcry. The PSP newspaper *Hoy* had just restarted publication and the fare increase gave the Communists an immediate popular cause to champion, as well as giving principled militants on the buses a feeling of popular support in their opposition to Marco Hirigoyen, the ARG leader of the Havana busworkers' union.[156] The ARG bureaucracy of the transport union was very strongly in favour of the fare increase, seeing it as an increase in revenue that they could plunder. Indeed, pressure from the ARG is the only explanation why Prío allowed such an unpopular measure to be enacted less than a year from a general election. But it was the students union, the *Federación de Estudiantes Universitarios* (FEU - Federation of University Students) which led the popular campaign with mass meetings and demonstrations, some numbering up to 100,000 participants.[157] The crisis was made worse when the police brutally assaulted a young *Ortodoxo* worker, Carlos Rodríguez, who was demonstrating against the fare increase. He later died of his injuries.[158] Meanwhile the government links with the ARG were made even clearer when Marco Hirigoyen, who had been arrested on a charge of illegal possession of firearms, was released after official intervention.[159] The fare increase was quietly dropped on a Sunday, the 16th September.[160]

---

155 U.S. Embassy Havana, Despatch 570 (3 October 1951) *Summary of Labor Developments During First Half of 1951*
156 *Hoy* (31 August 1951)
157 *Hoy* (6 September 1951)
158 *Hoy* (7 September 1951)
159 U.S. Embassy Havana, Despatch 408 (7 September, 1951) *FEU, Ortodoxos, Communists protest bus fare increase; Marco A. Hirigoyen and Manuel Pacin Guerra arrested under Gangsterism Law*
160 *El Mundo* (16 September 1951)

Coup

The main political winner from this debacle was the *Ortodoxo* party and a January 1952 poll by the news magazine *Bohemia* put them 12 points ahead of the *Autenticos* in the upcoming presidential election, with Batista trailing behind. An *Ortodoxo* victory was Prío's main fear, as they had promised to investigate his financial activities, so he ignored all the warnings he received of Batista's intended coup and then did nothing to oppose the military take-over on the morning of 10th March 1952.[161] The ARG had intended to murder Batista when he returned to the country at the beginning of 1951, but Prío had intervened and sent a message of reassurance to Batista saying that if anyone killed him it would give the presidency to the *Ortodoxos*.[162]

The main business newspaper, *Diario de la Marina* had been enthusiastically campaigning for Batista with a headline "*Batista es el Hombre*" (Batista is the Man). When Batista staged his coup, the US and British Embassies noted that businessmen were amongst the new regime's most enthusiastic supporters.[163] Within ten days of the coup, the major business associations had visited the presidential palace to offer their support.[164] The *Diario de la Marina* contrasted the situation under the previous government where the "*balance inclined monstrously toward the labour unions*", with the statements of the new government, which were described as "*serene and reasonable*".[165] The British Embassy, having noted "*the refreshing spectacle of an American dictator enjoying the support of ORIT*", was positively enthusiastic at the prospect that "*the Batista government will not be under the thumb of organised labour as their predecessors were*".[166] In fact Batista had quickly come to an understanding with Mujal, who had half-heartedly called a general strike then, once Batista had assured him that he could maintain his control of the CTC, called it off before most workers had even heard about the proposed action. Mujal maintained his control of the CTC bureaucracy, with the backing of Batista's army and police where necessary, right up to the arrival of the Rebel Army in Havana in January 1959, when he had to quickly seek asylum in the Argentine Embassy.

One of the few groups of workers who did go on strike in protest at the

161 Pardrón & Betancourt, Batista, el golpe (2013) p.19
162 Pardrón & Betancourt, Batista, el golpe (2013) pp.79-81
163 U.S. Embassy Havana, Despatch 1561 (24 March 1952) *Recognition*
164 *Havana Post* (14, 15, 19 March 1952)
    El Mundo (14, 15, 19 March 1952)
165 *Havana Post* (16 March 1952)
166 FO 371/97516 - AK1015/11 (17 March 1952) *ORIT*
    FO 371/97516 - AK1015/13 (21 March 1952) *Recognition*

Batista coup was the Havana public transport workers. Marco Hirigoyen was clearly unsatisfied with the change of regime and with his loss of influence; Batista did not need a gang of armed thugs to enforce his will, he had the Army and Police, who had given him the Presidency and who would show themselves more than prepared to use whatever violence was necessary against recalcitrant trade unionists. In May 1952, a secret US diplomatic report speaks of Batista's intelligence service telling the US Embassy that Hirigoyen was seeking an opportunity to oppose the regime and in early June he was openly speaking at union meetings of the need for a strike.[167] At the end of June, not having been paid for two weeks, the drivers' union conducted a publicity campaign aimed at winning the support of their passengers and were clearly preparing for a fight. On the other side, the government was talking publicly about slashing the subsidy required to continue the operations of *Autobuses Modernos*, the bus company for whom Hirigoyen worked.[168]

On 28th June, with no warning, soldiers occupied the bus termini and union office, Marco Hirigoyen and a number of other union delegates were arrested. The army confiscated the papers of every driver they could find and eight hundred out of the company's 7000 employees were dismissed.[169] Mujal, for whom Hirigoyen had served his purpose and was becoming a potential rival, protested meekly, but did nothing.[170] The British Ambassador, rejoicing at the army's intervention, wrote that *Autobuses Modernos*, "*had from the point of view of graft, rank inefficiency and financial loss become a crying scandal*".[171] With a nice touch of irony, Hirigoyen was charged with the murder of the Communist bus driver Manuel Montoro.[172]

The US government was also not particularly happy about Batista. The British government was bemused by the length of time it took for the USA to recognise the new Batista government but, from the US point of view, they had ended up with a dictator who, in 1944, they had already told not to stand again.[173] They were clearly not sure of his relationship with the Communist party, remembering the two government ministers from his previous presidency.[174] Given his known

---

167 U.S. Embassy Havana, Memorandum (15 May 1952)
    Bohemia (15 June 1952) "Autobuses"
168 *Bohemia* (29 June 1952)
169 U.S. Embassy Havana, Despatch 15 (3 July 1952) *Army occupied Autobuses Modernos*
    Bohemia (6 July 1952) "El 'Madrugon' de los Autobuses"
170 *Bohemia* (6 July 1952) "Autobuses"
171 FO 371/97516 - AK1015/33 (19 May 1952) - *Political Situation in Cuba*
172 *Bohemia* (6 July 1952) "Autobuses"
173 FO 371/97516 - AK1015/9 (13 March 1952) *Events surrounding the coup d'etat by General Batista*
174 U.S. Embassy Havana, Despatch 1561 (24 March 1952) *Recognition*

relationship with Mafia figures such as Meyer Lansky and Santo Trafficante, it was also unlikely that anything would be done to reduce the level of crime and corruption that was harming legitimate US business interests.[175] The US intelligence community seems to have outsourced the anti-Communist campaign in Cuba to the AFL, merely providing encouragement, finance and a post-bag via the embassy. The AFL then worked with local right-wing, corrupt trade union bureaucrats, who in turn collaborated with the Cuban government and local gangsters, all of whom had their own agendas and their own pockets to fill. The outcome was a complete mess and a public scandal. This led the army to take control before the *Ortodoxos* won an election and opened the lid of the whole can of worms. Had the *Ortodoxos* gained access to the papers detailing the corruption of the *Autentico* years they would doubtless have found much more corruption and murder. Unfortunately, the only candidate for dictator was himself hardly ideal, being as corrupt as the *Autentico* politicians he replaced and tainted by his previous role in government. Under Batista's rule the activities of the local gangsters were curbed and he quickly restored the "State Monopoly of Violence". Later, when Batista himself set up death squads in 1957 in an attempt to contain the growing rebellion against his dictatorship, he would not use gangsters, rather he gave the job to soldiers and policemen in plain clothes.

Shambles

The anti-Communist campaign in Cuba that started in 1947 was a shambles from the point of view of the Cuban ruling class, US capitalism and the Truman government. The US government had, in the early days of the Cold War, been concentrating its efforts on Europe. Jay Lovestone, sometime leader of the CP(USA) who had been expelled from the party when he lost a faction fight and turned into a rabid anti-Communist, was hired by the AFL to head the Free Trade Union Committee (FTUC), through which he organised the AFL's intervention as a conduit for CIA funds in the successful division of the French and Italian trade union federations.[176] The US state's intervention in Cuba was much less hands-on, there was no Marshall Plan to use as cover for their activities and there were Cubans who seemed determined to purge the trade unions with the ever willing aid of the AFL. As the saying goes: "Why have a dog and bark yourself?" The US Embassy kept a watching brief and acted as a postbox, but otherwise left matters to local anti-Communists and the AFL. However, such was the level of corruption

---

175 Cirules, *El imperio de La Habana* (1993) pp.39-43
    Colhoun, *Gangsterismo* (2013) pp.4-6
176 Morgan, *A Covert Life: Jay Lovestone: Communist, Anti-Communist and Spymaster* (1999)

in the Cuban ruling party, that the anti-Communist crusade was frequently jeopardised by the greed of its protagonists. So, by 1952, the US government had little choice but to give the go-ahead to Batista's coup. A study of US diplomatic correspondence shows that the possibility of an *Ortodoxo* election victory worried US business interests and their allies amongst the Cuban bourgeoisie.[177] The First National Bank of Boston led a syndicate that loaned the Cuban Government $200,000,000 to build such projects as the tunnel under Havana Bay.[178] This loan met with huge internal opposition in Cuba and the *Ortodoxos* made it quite clear that, if elected, they would not repay the debt.[179] Yet it was the widespread public revulsion against government corruption and links with gangsters that seemed likely to give electoral victory to the *Ortodoxos*, a victory that could threaten the considerable US investment in Cuba. Thus, when Dean Acheson, US Secretary of State, gave Jorge "Yoyo" García Montes the message for Batista that President Truman had authorised the coup, it was in many ways an admission of the failure of their previous strategy in Cuba.[180]

William Pawley, as well as running Autobuses Modernos, was a long serving member of the US intelligence community and, in 1954, his friend President Eisenhower appointed him to a "panel of consultants to conduct a study of the covert activities of the Central Intelligence Agency".[181] This panel was set up on Pawley's suggestion when he discovered, through his involvement in the group planning the overthrow of the government of Guatemalan President Jabob Arbenz, that internal opponents of the CIA's involvement in this plot were leaking details of the operation to the press. He used his position on this commission to bolster the position of his friend Allen Dulles and those CIA agents who favoured increased use of "Dirty Tricks". He went on to be involved in the planning of the US intervention in Guatemala. While it made some use of the AFL and it is known that Serafino Romualdi was in Guatemala at the time of the US sponsored invasion, this operation came directly under the control of the CIA. It may be that the experience of the mess made by the amateur anti-Communist efforts of the AFL, as observed by Pawley, convinced the CIA that outsourcing of such business was not advisable. He had certainly seen how the use of corrupt politicians and gangsters had interfered with the ability of US capitalists to do business and one of the considerations of the CIA intervention in Guatemala was to protect the

---

177 Alzugaray, *Crónica de un fracaso imperial* (2008) p.72-78
   U.S. Embassy Havana, Despatch 1994, (30 March 1951) *Eduardo Chibas lack of balance*
178 Ameringer, *The Cuban Democratic Experience* (2000) p.107
179 U.S. Embassy Havana, Despatch 1575 (26 January 1951) *Eduardo Chibas*
180 Pardrón & Betancourt, *Batista, el golpe* (2013) p.19
181 United States Department of State, *Letter From President Eisenhower to General James H. Doolittle,* (26 July 1954)

interests of US multinationals. The AFL, and subsequently the AFL-CIO following the merger with the Congress of Industrial Organisations (CIO) in 1955, went on to support many US government interventions from the coup in Chile in 1973 to the attempted coup in Venezuela in 2002. Nevertheless, they have never again been given such a free hand and were always restricted to a supporting role.

If it is hardly surprising to find the US government authorising coups and murders in Latin America, the sorry role of the American Federation of Labor perhaps requires more explanation. All union organisation has a tendency to bureaucratisation, with the organisation itself becoming more important to the people who run it than the original reason for which it was established. Moreover, an organisation based on "trade" unionism, with the emphasis on protecting the narrow craft interests of a skilled membership, will not have the counteracting pressure of a wider working class solidarity. The AFL operated in a context that became known as "business unionism"; the trade union was in the business of supplying and controlling skilled labour in partnership with the employers who supplied the capital. Local organisers of the AFL were known as "business agents" and the undemocratic nature of the Federation gave these bureaucrats plenty of scope for corruption. Therefore, Mafia involvement in "Labor Racketeering" is unsurprising.

In situations like this, the trade union bureaucracy fears radicals of any description much more than it fears the employers. Operating within the *status quo* and completely accepting the capitalist system, the AFL felt the need to show its patriotism. The AFL leadership saw the state as a neutral entity, above class differences and they sought to gain influence by assisting where there is a perceived common interest with the state. Collaboration during the Second World War, justified as defence of democracy and opposition to fascism, set a pattern which, in the context of the Cold War, easily turned into anti-communism and found no difficulty employing notorious spies such as Serafino Romualdi and Jay Lovestone, particularly as there was ample funding available as a spin off from the Marshall Plan, not all of which had to be spent for the purposes for which it had been allocated. In the early years of this century, unions in California have called for the AFL-CIO to open their archives and reveal the full history of the federation's foreign activities. The AFL-CIO International Affairs Department has consistently refused to allow its own members access to this information.

Conclusion

During the Second World War, the AFL leadership predicted the coming Cold War and attempted to position themselves favourably by supporting local efforts to sow divisions in the Cuban labour movement and thereby develop an international base for the forthcoming anti-Communist assault on the whole Latin American labour movement. However, while the take-over of the CTC was apparently successful, the greed, violence and corruption of their Cuban allies made for a scandal that seriously undermined their usefulness to the US government and, as a result, the AFL was reduced to a minor supporting role in future anti-Communist activities.

There was another reason why the murderous intervention in the CTC was a shambles. The Cuban workers' movement proved much more resilient than expected. In 1947, the Communist leadership of the CTC had renounced the overt class collaboration associated with Browderism, but the daily practice of the union leadership had been much slower to react. The murder of some the more militant and honest leaders of the CTC forced a speedy reassessment of the situation. The violent assault on militants was a blow, but one from which the movement recovered remarkably quickly as new leaders appeared. We know the names of some of them, many more operated in a clandestine fashion and must remain anonymous. As access to the official trade union machinery was largely denied them, these emerging leaders proved effective in creating new structures, networks and committees to replace the old structures. Thus, when Batista staged his coup, working class networks of resistance were already in place and would go on to play an important role in his eventual overthrow. This was not quite what the murderers of Jesús Menéndez and Arecelio Iglesias had in mind.

Biographical Details

Francisco Aguirre (1910-1960). Leader of of the restaurant workers' federation and Organising Secretary of the CTC. An *Autentico* congressman, he served as Minster of Labour in 1947-48. Secretary of CIT and then ORIT. Died in prison in Cuba in the early 1960s.

José Alemán (1903-1950). Minister of Education during the Grau government. Paid gangsters from the funds of the Ministry. Amassed a fortune of $200 million during his term as minister.

Juán Arévalo (died 1948). Leader of the *Federación de Obreros Marítimos Nacional* (FOMN - National Federation of Maritime Workers). Independent Social Democrat. Initial contact between the anti-Communist faction in the CTC and the AFL using his role as Secretary for Foreign Relations of the CTC. Murdered, probably by Emilio Surí Castillo (see below).

Fulgencio Batista y Zaldívar (1901 - 1973). President of Cuba from 1940-1944. Seized power again in 1952 and instituted a dictatorship that was overthrown in 1959.

Earl Browder (1891 - 1973). General Secretary of the CP(USA) 1930-1945. Stood for a policy of reconciliation between communism and capitalism known as *Browderism*. Expelled from the CP(USA) in 1946.

Hector Cabrera (died 1948). Bus driver and rank and file Communist, killed by ARG gunmen while in conversation with colleagues at the terminus on 11th April 1948.

Manuel Campanería Rojas. *Mujalista* head of the *Federación Tabacalera Nacional* (FTN National). Murderer of Miguel Fernández Roig (see below).

Eduardo "Eddie" Chibás (1907- 1951). Founder of the *Ortodoxo* party in 1947. Senator and campaigner against corruption.

Angel Cofiño. General Secretary of the *Federación Eléctrica* (Electrical Workers' Federation) and leader of the *Comisión Obrera Nacional Independiente* (CON-I). General Secretary of the CTC 1947 to 1949 when he was replaced by Eusebio Mujal (see below).

Carlos Febles (died 1948). A Communist bus driver who was active in the campaign to oppose the proposed fare increase. On 20th October 1948 he was shot dead while sleeping on his bus at the terminus.

Eufemio Fernández. Leader of *Acción Revolucionaria Guiteras* (ARG) which did much of the dirty work of killing *unitario* CTC leaders. Served as head of the *Policía Secreta Nacional* (National Secret Police) during Carlos Prío's Presidency.

Miguel Fernández Roig (1894 - 1948). Tobacco worker and founder member of the Cuban Communist Party. General Secretary of the tobacco workers' union in the 1920s and 1930s. *Secretario de Organización del Sindicato de Torcedores de La Habana* (Organising Secretary of the Havana Cigar Rollers Union) and union secretary in La Corona cigar works where he was attacked and killed by a gang led by Manuel Campanería Rojas (see above), *mujalista* head of the *Federación Tabacalera Nacional* (FTN National Federation of Tobacco Workers).

William Z. Foster (1881 - 1961). Trade union organiser and Chairman of the CP(USA) from 1924 - 34 and 1945 - 57.

Jesús González Cartas (aka *El Extraño*). A leading member of the ARG. President Prío appointed him *Jefe de la Policía Marítima del Puerto de La Habana* (Chief of the Maritime Police of the Port of Havana). He was widely believed to be personally implicated in the murders of *unitario* trade unionists but was protected by his links to the presidential palace where he was a frequent visitor.

Ramón Grau San Martín (1881 - 1969). President of Cuba (1933-1934 and 1944-1948).

Gilberto Goliath. *Mujalista* General Secretary of the *Federación Obrera Maritima Nacional* (FOMN, National Maritime Workers' Federation).

Samuel Gompers (1850-1924). Cigar maker and founding leader of the AFL. Set the AFL firmly in the practice of "Business Unionism".

Antonio Guiteras (1906 - 1935). A leading opponent of the Machado dictatorship in the 1930s He had briefly served as Minister of the Interior during the 1933 revolution and was responsible for many reforms such as the minimum wage. Killed in the re-pression following the defeat of the 1935 general strike.

Marco Hirigoyen. A member of the ARG who used this wave of assassinations to remove his political opponents and take over the transport union. From this base he se-cured a place on the executive of the CTC. Supported Eusebio Mujal (see below) against Angel Cofiño (see above) for CTC General Secretary in 1949. In 1952, he was arrested by for murder of the Communist bus driver Manuel Montoro (see below) but allowed to go into exile.

Aracelio Iglesias (1901-1948). Dock worker, trade union leader and Communist militant. Secretary of the *Sindicato de Estibadores y Jornaleros de la Bahia de La Habana* (Union of Stevedores and Labourers of the Bay of Havana) and the National Executive of the *Federación Obrera Maritima Nacional* (FOMN, National Maritime Workers' Federation) as well as the National Executive of the CTC. He was murdered on 17th October 1948 by gangsters linked to CON(A).

Meyer Lansky (1902 -1983). Senior member of the Mafia resident in Havana. Known to work with the US Office of Naval Intelligence. Close associate of Fulgencio Batista.

Anton Lezcano (died 1947). Bus driver. Shot by police on 27th October 1947 while protesting against the Ministry of Labour intervention in the transport workers' union. Died on 12th November.

Vicente Lombardo Toledano (1894-1968). Mexican trade union leader. Founder and head of the *Confederación de Trabajadores de América Latina* (CTAL - Workers Confederation of Latin America). Communist "Fellow Traveller" but never a member of the Party.

Lucky Luciano (1897 - 1962). Founder of modern organised crime in the USA. Released from prison and deported following wartime collaboration with the US Office of Naval Intelligence, he returned to Cuba in 1947 where he became friendly with Paco Prío (see below). Deported to Italy in 1948.

Evelio Lugo. Tobacco worker and leader of the *unitario* cigar workers' union organisation.

Jesús Menéndez (1911 - 1948). Cuban sugar worker, trade union leader and Communist political activist. General Secretary of the *Federación Nacional de los Trabajadores Azucareros* (FNTA, National Federation of Sugar Industry Workers) and executive member of the CTC. He was shot in the back by Captain Joaquín Casillas on Matanzas railway station, while he was touring the country building support for a strike. The order for the assassination was given by the Chief of the Army General Staff. His funeral in Havana was attended by 150,000 people.

Manuel Montoro (died 1947). A bus driver and leading Communist activist, shot down in a café by gunmen from *Acción Revolucionaria Guiteras* (ARG) on 10th November 1947

Eusebio Mujal (1915-1986). Cuban Senator and member of the *Partido Autodoxo*. General Secretary of the CTC from 1949-1959 following the 1947 purges. Important figure in the anti-Communist trade union federations CIT and ORIT. Renowned for his corruption and greed, he played an important role in supporting the Batista dictatorship from 1952-1959.

José Oviedo (died 1949). Communist sugar worker shot and killed in a gangster attack on a union mass meeting on 18th September 1949, in *Central Francisco* in Camagüey province.

Lázaro Peña (1911-1974). Cigar worker and trade union leader. General Secretary of the CTC from 1939-1947. Leader and figurehead of the PSP's trade union activity following the purges. In 1953, he went into exile to Prague where he worked as vice-president of the World Federation of Trade Unions. He returned to Cuba in 1959 immediately after the revolutionary victory and was elected General Secretary of the CTC in 1961 and to the Central Committee of the *Partido Comunista de Cuba* (Cuban Communist Party) in 1965.

Félix Palú (died 1947). Member of CON(A) killed in raid on the textile workers union in the lead up to the V Congress of the CTC while attempting to seize the conference papers.

Antonio Prío Socarrás (1905-1990). A Cuban banker and Finance Minister during his brother's Presidency when he was accused of embezzling considerable sums from union pension funds.

Carlos Prío Socarrás (1903-1977). During the Grau administration he was Minister of Public Works, Minister of Labour and Prime Minister. He was Minister of Labour during the 1947 purges. President from 1948-1952, when he was deposed by Fulgencio Batista in a coup.

Francisco "Paco" Prío Socarrás (1902-1988). From 1944 to 1952, he was a Senator representing Pinar del Rio province He was a drug dealer and a gambler, a close friend of the Mafia bosses, Mayer Lansky and Lucky Luciano.

Amancio Rodríguez (died 1949). Communist sugar worker shot and killed in a gangster attack on a union mass meeting on 18th September 1949, in *Central Francisco* in Camagüey province.

Conrado Rodriguez. Provincial sugar workers' leader from Las Villas. Campaigned against the theft of money from workers' pension funds.

Ricardo Rodriguez. General Secretary of the *Hermandad Ferroviaria* (Railway Brotherhood). Purged in 1947 and continued his trade activities in the Ciénaga railway yards. Arrested for possession of explosives in 1957. Member of the *Partido Socialista Popular* (PSP).

Ursinio Rojas (1913 - 1994). Sugar worker and Communist militant. Replaced Jesús Menéndez (see above) as leader of the *unitario* sugar workers. Negotiated an alliance with Fidel Castro on behalf of the PSP in 1958. Member of the Central Committee of the Cuban Communist Party from 1965.

Serafino Romualdi (1900 -1967). Latin American representative of the AFL. Phillip Agee described him as the "*principal CIA agent for labour operations in Latin America*". Worked closely with the anti-Communist faction in the CTC.

Pablo Sandoval. Replaced Aracelio Iglesias (see above) as leader of the *unitario* dockers in the Port of Havana.

Julián Sotolongo. Sugar worker and *unitario* leader of the *Federación de Trabajadores de la Provincia de Camagüey* until removed from office by government intervention in 1948. Worked as clandestine organiser in *Camagüey* until the revolutionary victory in 1959.

Emilio Surí Castillo (died 1951). Secretary of the *Comisión Obrera Nacional Auténtica* (CON(A) - National Workers' Commission of the *Autentico* Party), a leading member of the *Federación Nacional de Trabajadores Azucareros* (FNTA - National Federation of Sugar Workers) and CTC Correspondence Secretary. A long history of violence against political opponents, he was personally implicated in the murder of several *unitario* trade unionists. Killed in a car crash.

Juan Taquechel (1908 - 2002). Communist dockworker from Santiago de Cuba. Secretary General of the *Federación General de Trabajadores de Oriente* (FGTO General Federation of Workers in Oriente Province). Removed from post by police on the instruction of the Ministry of Labour in February 1948. Organised a dock strike in support of the armed uprising in Santiago in November 1956.

Bibliography

Archives in Havana, Cuba

    Instituto de Historia de Cuba (IHC)
    Archivo Nacional Cubana (ANC)
    Biblioteca Nacional "José Martí"

Provincial Archives in Cuba

    Archivo Provincial de Las Villas, Santa Clara
    Archivo Provincial de Camagüey
    Archivo Historico de Sancti Spiritus

Personal Collections in Cuba

    Angelina Rojas, of the Insituto de Historia de Cuba

Archives in UK

    British National Archives – Kew

        [References to archival material to be found in the British National Archive at Kew will be given starting with the folder reference, where FO 371 refers to records created and inherited by the Foreign Office. This is followed by the document reference. Reports from Labour Attachés start LAB/13 and do not have individual document numbers, but are identified by date]

    British Library
    London School of Economics Library

        [for "US Confidential State Department Central Files 1945-49" reels 11 and 12, numbered 837.504]

Books and Articles

Agee, Phillip, 1975, *Inside the Company: CIA Diary,* Harmondsworth: Penguin.

Ameringer, Charles, 2000, *The Cuban Democtaric Experience: the Auténtico Years, 1944-1952* Gainesville, Florida: University Press of Florida.

Bethell, Leslie & Roxborough, Ian, 1988, "Latin America between the Second World War and the Cold War, 1944-1948", *Journal of Latin American Studies*, Cambridge: Cambridge University Press vol.20 no.1, May, p.167-189.

Buchanan, Paul G., 1990, "Useful Fools as Diplomatic Tools: Organized Labor as an Instrument of US Foreign Policy In Latin America", *Kellog Institute Working Paper*, no.136, April

Canton Navarro, José, 2013, *Cuba bajo el signo de la Segunda Guerra Mondial* La Habana: Editoria Historia.

Canton Navarro, José, 1977, *Aracelio Iglesias* Havana: Editorial Arte y Literatura

Carew, Anthony, 2010, "The American Labor Movement in Fizzland: The Free Trade Union Committee and the CIA", *Labor History*, p.25-42.

Carew, Anthony, 1987, *Labour Under the Marshall Plan: The Politics of Productivity and the Marketing of Management Science* Manchester: Manchester University Press

Cirules, Enrique, 1993, *El imperio de La Habana* Havana: Casa de las Américas.

Colhoun, Jack, 2013, *Gangsterismo, The United States, Cuba, and the Mafia: 1933 to 1966* London: OR Books.

Duarte Hurtado, Martín, 1973, *La maquina torcedora de tabaco y las luchas en torno a su implementación en Cuba* Havana: Ciencias Sociales.

Duclos, Jacques, 1945, "On the Dissolution of the Communist Party of the United States", *Cahiers du Communisme*, April.

García Galló, Gaspar Jorge, 1998, *General de las cañas* Havana: Editora política.

Hughes, Quenby Olmsted, 2011, *In the Interest of Democracy: the rise and fall of the early Cold War alliance between the American Federation of Labor and the Central Intelligence Agency* Oxford: Peter Lang.

Kofas, Jon V., 1992, *The Struggle for Legitimacy : Latin American Labor and the United States, 1930-1960* Tempe: Center for Latin American Studies, Arizona State University.

Moore, Barrington, 1945, "The Communist Party of the USA: An Analysis of a Social Movement", *The American Political Science Review*, vol.39 no.1, February, p.31-41.

Morgan, Ted, 1999, *A Covert Life: Jay Lovestone: Communist, Anti-Communist and Spymaster* New York: Random House.

Pardrón, José Luis & Betancourt, Luis Adrián, 2013, *Batista, el golpe* Havana: Ediciones Unión.

Partido Comunista De Cuba (PCC), Instituto de Historia del Movimiento Comunista y de la Revolución Socialista de Cuba, 1985, *Historia del movimiento obrero cubano, tomo II* Havana: Editora Política.

Pérez Pérez, Angel, 1974, *La huelga de 55 en el Central Estrella* Havana: Departament de Orinetación Revolucionaria del Partido Comunista de Cuba.

Rojas Blaquier,Angelina, 1998, *1955 - Crónica de una marcha ascendente,* Havana: Instituto de Historia de Cuba.

Rojas Blaquier, Angelina, 2006, *El Primer Partido Comunista de Cuba 1935 - 1952, tomo 2* Santiago de Cuba: Editorial Oriente.

Romualdi, Serafino, 1967, *Presidents and Peons : Recollections of a Labor Ambassador in Latin America* New York: Funk & Wagnalls.

Romualdi, Serafino, 1947, "Labor and Democracy in Latin America", *Foreign Affairs*, vol.25 no.1-4, April, p.477.

Roxborough, Ian, 1994 "Labor Control and the Postwar Growth Model in Latin America", in Rock, David (ed.), *Latin America in the 1940's: War and Postwar Transitions*, Berkley: University of California Press.

Ryan, James Gilbert, 1977, "The Making of a Native Marxist: The Early Career of Earl Browder", *The Review of Politics*, vol.39 no.3, p.332-362.

Scipes, Kim, 2005, "Labor Imperialism Redux? The AFL-CIO's Foreign Policy Since 1995", *Monthly Review*, vol.57 no.1, May.

Sims, Harold, 1992 "Cuba", in Bethell, Leslie & Roxborough, Ian (ed.), *Latin America between the Second World War and the Cold War, 1944-1948*, Cambridge: Cambridge University Press.

Sims, Harold Dana, 1991, "Collapse of the House of Labor", *Cuba Studies*, no.21, p.123-147.

Stubbs, Jean, 1985, *Tobacco on the Periphery : a case study in Cuban labour history, 1860-1958*, Cambridge: Cambridge University Press.

Tellería Toca, Evelio, 1973, *Congresos obreros en Cuba*, Havana: Instituto Cubano del Libro.

Tennant, Gary, 1999, *Dissident Cuban Communism: The Case of Trotskyism, 1932-1965* University of Bradford PhD thesis.

Toth, Charles W., 1967, "Samuel Gompers, Communism, and the Pan American Federation of Labor", *The Americas*, vol.23 no.3, January, p.273-278.

Truslow, Francis Adams, 1951, *Report on Cuba* Washington, D.C.: International Bank for Reconstruction and Development.

Whitney, Robert, 2001, *State and Revolution in Cuba*, Chapel Hill: University of North Carolina Press.

Yanike, L. Lee, 1986, *US Confidential State Department Central Files 1945-49* Frederick, MD: University Publications of America.

Zanetti, Oscar & García, Alejandro, 1987, *Caminos para el azúcar* Havana: Editorial de Ciencias Sociales.

The Socialist History Society

The Socialist History Society was founded in 1992 and includes many leading Socialist and labour historians, academic and amateur researchers, in Britain and overseas. The SHS holds regular events, public meeting controversies. We produce a range of publications, including the journal Socialist History and a regular Newsletter.

The SHS is the successor to the Communist Party History Group, which was established in 1946 and is now totally independent of all political parties and groups. We are engaged in and seek to encourage historical studies from a Marxist and broadly-defined left perspective. We are interested in all aspects of human history from the earliest social formations to the present day and aim for an international approach.

We are particularly interested in the various struggles of labour, of women, of progressive campaigns and peace movements around the world, as well as the history of colonial peoples, black people, and all oppressed communities seeking justice, human dignity and liberation.

Each year we produce two issues of our journal Socialist History, one or two historical pamphlets in our Occasional Publications series, and frequent members' Newsletters. We hold public lectures and seminars mainly in London. In addition, we hold special conferences, book launches and joint events with other friendly groups.

Join the Socialist History Society today!

Members receive all our serial publications for the year at no extra cost and regular mailings about our activities. Members can vote at our AGM and seek election to positions on the committee, and are encouraged to participate in other society activities.

Annual membership fees for 2017 (renewable every January):

> Full UK £25.00
> Concessionary UK £18.00
> Europe full £30.00
> Europe concessionary £24.00
> Rest of world full £35.00
> Rest of world concessionary £29.00

For details of institutional subscriptions, please e-mail the treasurer on francis@socialisthistorysociety.co.uk.

To join the society for 2017, please send your name and address plus a cheque/PO payable to Socialist History Society to: SHS, 50 Elmfield Road, Balham, London SW17 SAL. You can also pay online.

Visit our websites on www.socialisthistorysociety.co.uk and www.socialist-history-journal.org.uk.